EXTRAORDINARY

INSPIRING STORIES OF LIVING AND LOVING BEYOND THE LABEL

CARMEL CHARLESWORTH   CHRISTINE MCTIGHE

GINA COOPER   HERMELINDA SIMON

JESS MUNKS   KAREN BAKER   LARA WILLIAMS

LYSANDRA CALLAHAN   MASON DAMIAN

MEL WANGMANN   MISTY COY SNYDER

NICHOLE DUREGON   NYREE JOHNSON

RACHEL CALLANDER   GEORGIA HANSEN

gm
House

CONTENTS

This book is dedicated to the extraordinary souls who are our shining lights that watch over and have guided this journey from heaven.

Amelia, Georgia's daughter who was full term stillborn in 2017.

Ruby, Gina's daughter who was born still at 32 weeks in 2022.

Lysandra's four angels Kasey, Chiara, Blake and Jake.

Evie, Rachel's daughter who died at 2.5 years old in 2010.

INTRODUCTION

I remember the exact moment when the idea for this book landed in my heart. I was driving up the mountain on my favourite Sunday family ritual. We often drive through the beautiful rainforest of Mount Tamborine and get ice cream and coffee.

This particular day I was enjoying the view and fresh mountain rainforest air as we drove, which always grounds me and evokes a sense of wonder and peace, when this idea dropped with a power so fierce, it needed to have action taken on it straight away.

I messaged my dear soul sister Lara and shared with her my vision - to create a collaborative book, with inspiring stories of others moving through stories and journeys like she was experiencing, with her beautiful baby Bonnie (see Lara's story on page 79)

She met my message and idea with nonchalance, almost like she hadn't even read the message (which I know she did). She wasn't ignorant, or dismissive or anything like that, it's literally like the idea wasn't ready to land in her consciousness yet. I wasn't bothered at all. I just knew if it was meant to be, it would be when the timing was divine.

A few days later when we were chatting, the idea popped into my awareness again, and so I brought it up again. This time, her interest was piqued. As if hearing it for the first time, it was like her voice lit up. And I knew in that moment, the idea landed in her too.

A week later, we met to talk through all of the ideas, details and excitement of the idea wanting to birth through us.

And so began the birth of this Extraordinary book into the world.

The stories in this book examine the essence of the human spirit, human connection and communication.

It is so uncanny to me, that amongst them all, unknowing to each other, there are similar themes and messages.

One is this theme of how we communicate as humans, and those who are different or special, with a disability or diagnosis, have this extraordinary ability to communicate beyond words, like a sixth sense. It's a communication between bodies, beyond the traditional realm of language. They use their eyes, their souls, their innate spirit or essence to express themselves, and in doing so, there is this opportunity to see beyond their physical body.

The other message is even more profound and powerful for me personally. When my daughter died in 2017, just weeks later, I had the intuitive message that I would be publishing a book with the message to *Light the Way*. At that time, I wasn't a publisher, or an author and although it's akin to my skillset, I had no idea that would be my path.

As I read the stories in this book, it occurred to me that almost every author referred to lighting the way through their experience. Some even used the exact words!

This was divine confirmation to me of what I've believed for some time.

We are all connected. Everything is divinely orchestrated and timed.

My hope and desire for you in reading these stories, is that you receive the messages, the nuggets of wisdom within these stories. That these extraordinary humans leave you feeling hopeful on your darkest days, empowered to live a full and rich life regardless of what you might be facing or experiencing.

Please remember, wherever you are, whatever you're experiencing, it's all happening for reasons, sometimes beyond your comprehension, FOR you. Let there be hope. Let there be wonder. Let there be Grace and magic in all of it.

We trusted, from the beginning, this book would be a collection of stories from the exact extraordinary humans we were meant to share and illuminate.

And so it is.

And it is so.

With love,

Georgie

"The difference between ordinary and extraordinary is that litte EXTRA"-
Jimmy Johnson

UNION OF PURPOSE

A sking my husband to pinch me hard on the side of my torso was never something I imagined doing. It's a sensitive area for me at the best of times. But I did, and he agreed; grudgingly. It was a scientific experiment. I waited for that pain to register, but it didn't. Nothing happened. I could feel pressure there, but no pain. He tried another area on my torso with the same result. I asked him to pinch my upper arm like he did on my torso - THAT hurt and left a bruise the next day. Such a simple test confirmed something was wrong. I knew it wasn't normal, and so began my medical journey.

I've always been into sports. Growing up, we were never far from a sporting ground, squash court or walking track. On family days, a backyard game of cricket was always on the cards. Despite my active lifestyle, I struggled with my weight. It's been a lifelong battle. Until recently, my New Year's resolutions always revolved around weight loss and reaching a goal weight. That golden number, I believed, would magically make me love my body. It took me many years to realise that self-love doesn't work like that.

Cue lightbulb moment here. Self-love isn't a destination you arrive at, like a travel destination. It's travelling along the same roads and seeing the sights differently the first, second and third time. It's understanding and acceptance of self regardless of which detour you make or dead end you find yourself at. Self-love is the journey of learning and evolving with each new version of yourself. Gaining a deeper connection to who you truly are and what brings you joy.

I sought a counsellor about eight years ago to assist me with exploring my conditioning and belief systems. I didn't want to be at war with myself anymore. I was tired of always wanting to achieve a better version of myself, which involved shedding what I thought wasn't good enough for everyone else. I didn't feel worthy. I didn't love myself for who I was, but I desperately wanted to. My inner work during those sessions opened my eyes to so much. I listened to my emotions for the first time and understood where the triggers came from. The learned patterns came to the surface, and I felt liberated in allowing them, addressing them and letting them go. I was also more aware of my body physically. She had carried and birthed two beautiful boys and deserved love, recognition and kindness.

I realised that my body is the best communicator; she always told me what she needed. Up until then, I hadn't been paying attention. I suffered a lot from headaches and took painkillers daily, sometimes several times a day. I had regular massages to release muscle tension, which only helped a little. After two months of this, I went to my GP. He was concerned about the length of time my headaches had lasted and ordered some tests. After a few weeks of appointments, the doctors concluded I clench my jaw too much, creating headaches. All I could do that I wasn't already doing was chew gum whilst working at my desk to relax my jaw. It helped slightly, but it never went away completely.

Brisbane's cooler temperatures arrived in June 2021, and my boys started playing winter sports again. I enjoyed volunteering as a Sports Trainer to ensure player welfare in their Rugby League teams. At the start of the week, my hands were constantly cold, as they usually are, but the tips of my fingers felt numb also. With the change in weather, I didn't think too much of it at the time. However, Sunday, game day arrived, and the altered sensation hadn't gone away. I remember jogging onto the field to assist an injured player and it felt like my feet had gone to sleep. It wasn't a pleasant feeling. My concentration went from the player to focused on the ground watching where I was running. I desperately wanted to jog normally and not fall over in front of the players and spectators.

Later that night, after having a shower, I was drying myself and stopped when I came to dry my torso. I ran the towel over my stomach, specifically the section in between my breasts and belly button and felt little of that movement. I did the same section around my sides and my back, nothing. I watched the towel glide in the mirror, but what I saw and felt were not the same. I confessed to my husband that something weird was happening, explaining my symptoms. He ran his fingers over my stomach and back to test what I just told him. Then we did the pinching experiment. He was concerned, and at that moment, I was too. We discussed the other symptoms I had had leading up to this moment, and it occurred to me there was another one. Most of us have had the experience of being asked a question upon just waking up, especially with children in the home. Your mind reaches for that word or answer that you know but can't push to the forefront of your mind. It's just out of your grasp and on the tip of your tongue. When this started happening more regularly, I thought it was due to prolonged headaches and tiredness and busyness. Not being able to focus was extremely frustrating, as was having conversations with people and changing a word mid-sentence because you can't remember or pronounce it properly. It was not noticeable to others, but it was hard work and distressing. My husband noticed the slight change in the pauses and forgetfulness but never commented on it until I listed it as one of my symptoms.

Back to the GP. He had a hundred questions. The only two I answered yes to were – do you still have a headache, and is it numb here? They were the only two physical symptoms I had. He was concerned and referred me to a Consulting Physician who gave me the same set of questions. More tests - bloodwork, nerve testing and MRI. I did research external to the medical professionals who didn't want to give me a reason to panic. I respected that, but I also wanted to know all the

3

information, options and possibilities first to prepare. My research led me to three probable causes nerve damage, vitamin deficiency or MS.

In life, we so often dismiss the little things and don't think more than a second thought about them until we're forced to. Then, we look back at those little signs, hints and clues that now add up to the big picture that's staring right back at us. At the follow-up appointment, the Physician asked if I had researched my symptoms. I said I had. He asked what my findings led me to believe was going on. I explained my three possibilities. Finally, he said his opinion, he agreed that I have RRMS – active Multiple Sclerosis.

I was referred to a Neurologist to receive diagnosis confirmation, further information and possible treatments. I had new MRI scans to find any difference in the weeks between the first and current scans. There were differences. In that short time, little white dots lit up like bulbs on a Christmas tree through my neck and brain. Little scars where my body had felt an enemy invader present and tried to fight them off, not realising it was its own kind. These were the lesions causing my symptoms and potentially more serious ones if I didn't seek treatment.

Baseline - I heard that word more in the weeks after my diagnosis than I've ever thought possible outside watching Wimbledon. Between the tests I had done, I was also getting check-ups. Skin cancer checks, pap smear, eye tests, vaccinations, boosters, self-examinations. I needed to provide them with a baseline for all these things so we knew where the beginning was. The new normal started now. Changes happening here on in, we couldn't determine if it was a natural occurrence or some-thing accelerated by treatment and all had the potential to cause prob-lems in the future. My body's healing capabilities would be compromised, and as a result, my immune system would be suscep-tible to attack.

My research took the shock out of the equation when I received my diagnosis, but it didn't take away the other emotions, denial, anger, bargaining, and depression. I read that these stages are our attempts to process change and protect ourselves while we adapt to a new reality.

My new reality was unclear—much of it is out of my control. I grieved for my life as I knew it and my life as I imagined it. I grieved for my loved ones as I shared the news over the coming days. I grieved for my body as she was the one who had done the damage without even knowing it. I grieved for days. My boys didn't understand the implications of my diagnosis, but at the time, I was glad they were too young to ask the hard questions and the what-ifs. I told them about the things they would notice and what would affect our daily lives. Mum will get tired more quickly and have earlier nights. Don't drink out of Mum's water bottle after treatment. The whole family needs to help with the jobs around the house. Mum might need your help opening jars, carrying heavy items or picking up things she's dropped. All are small individually, but they add up to the bigger picture.

One experience that did surprise me was a sudden onset of body repulsion. I experienced body dissatisfaction when I was younger, but this was different and completely out of left field. I felt dirty. I felt like tainted and damaged goods. I knew my condition wasn't transmissible or a danger to others; I gave myself all the reasons why it wasn't rational to think that way and all the science to back that up, yet I still felt it and thought it. It felt like a a foreign entity that had been born from the situation I was in, and I didn't know what to make of it or why I couldn't shift it. The connection between my soul and body had been temporarily jaded, and all the work I had done to love myself unconditionally was rewritten with a new version installed. After some hard questions and self-reflection, I realised that it was another layer of grief that required healing.

It would be far easier to accept situations and experiences if healing was linear, but being the complex creatures we are, it's not possible. So I unpacked that little grief gift the same way I shifted my conditioning and belief systems; shone a light on it, acknowledged the fear, sat with it, meditated, cried, released, and breathed. Bit by bit, it lifted, but grief never leaves you entirely. It's always there in some form. The blessings that life gives us help us move through these challenges, and gratitude has always been a huge part of my attitude in life. I ask myself when experiencing these challenges – what am I learning from this? Growth happens in the shadows. Once you shine a light on it, you see it for what it is. It's uncomfortable, but that's where the magic is. After my tears had stopped, I remembered my journey of self-love. Acceptance. Forgiveness. Kindness. My body needed those now more than ever. I did a healing meditation and had a soul conversation with my physical body. To heal, we must move forward. I love you. I forgive you. I love you.

To anyone watching, they wouldn't notice my concentration while doing up buttons or strategically placing my hands under items to ensure it was balanced, and I wouldn't drop them. The numbness in my fingers has remained, but I've adapted. There's no other option for moving forward. I'm fortunate my first infusion treatment went well with nearly no side effects. At the end of the day, I was contemplating and reflecting. How blessed am I? If I have this diagnosis during my life, now is the absolute best time to have it. I've had my children, received comprehensive medical assistance, and my treatment is one of many developments that have been developed over decades of research, funding and awareness. My loved ones have supported me; we have our home, lives, and each other. And I'm here. I'm alive and owe it to myself and my family to make this work. I had faith that it was going to be ok.

My first thought was to remove what no longer aligned with me and keep what brings me joy. So, I was ready to move on after sixteen years of employment with the same company. I put my intention into action, calling forward a specific job description. I was still actively looking when I received my diagnosis until the fear of the unknown stopped me in my tracks. With the threat of a compromised immune system, I struggled to imagine taking on a new work environment with no paid annual leave or sick days available. There are so many unknowns and variables and many reasons to stay in the comfort zone. My decision to move forward ultimately came down to one factor – my happiness.

I wasn't happy or fulfilled. There was so much more I could offer the right company, and I knew it was there waiting for me. And so it was. I saw a job advertised which felt like it was written about me. Even the timing was perfect - interview Monday, role accepted Tuesday, resigned Thursday, and I took a four-week holiday over Christmas before starting. I hadn't had four weeks off in twenty years. It was the time I needed to reset, refocus, and reclaim my relationships—both with myself and my family. I didn't want to accept that my life wasn't in my control. That scared me more than anything. I have control over so much; I just needed to stop and look at where I was. Controlling your intentions and what you focus on is within your control. There may be other things outside your control, but intention and focus are yours to own. What you choose to do with those two blessings is up to you. It's yours. You have the power.

Extraordinary – Living and Loving Beyond The Label has enabled me to fulfil a life-long dream of becoming an author – albeit not with the same context I imagined. After meeting some of the authors and the background of their stories, I realised the enormity of this project and the power it will have for people around the world. That made me cry. I understood. I was reminded once again of the power of the words I speak. I voiced to my husband not long after my diagnosis that I would love to be an MS advocate and speaker to help others on their journey. There is magic in universal intentions.

My MS journey has been very private, and I've shared this new chapter of my life with very few people. I did want to share. There were so many occasions when I wanted to tell them. The thing I struggled with most was the reaction. Their grief. I felt that more than my own at times. I also didn't want my news to overshadow birthday celebrations or kill the mood of a lively dinner. I didn't feel that casually dropping it into the conversation was how I could share something so significant. Then the time came and went; the time in between seeing them grew longer, and I couldn't tell them. Sharing in this way, through my chapter, allows me to honour myself and use my journey to empower others going through their journey. I can't imagine a better union of purpose than that. I was fortunate to have known others living with MS and could reach out to them and ask real-life questions. The ones the doctors can't answer. Like any medical condition or diagnosis, you can't know what it's like unless you live it. With so much uncertainty, knowing that someone who understands is only a message or call away is invaluable. Their support and example showed me that this isn't a life sentence. You can live the life you want as long as you care for yourself. It was then that I also decided that because I'm not alone, I would work towards letting others with MS know that they're not alone either.

In September 2022, thirteen months after my initial diagnosis; I found out my current treatment is working. I'm so blessed I was diagnosed early. I'm so grateful that I trusted my intuition and listened to what my body told me. Get to know your body. Find out what cues it's giving you and why. Trust yourself and know what's going on for you. Only you will know. Put your health and wellbeing first – physically, mentally and spiritually.

Seek answers. Find your truth. MS is typically diagnosed between the ages of 20 – 40 and has many different symptoms, varying in number and severity. Currently, there is no cure, but many different treatments are available. You have options, and you are not alone on this journey.

CARMEL CHARLESWORTH

Carmel is an Authenticity Advocate who empowers others to see their beauty, showing them how to be their authentic selves, without fear or judgement.

Volunteering her time within the community as a Justice of the Peace and a Level 2 NRL Sports Trainer, she loves assisting people and embodies her core values of compassion with love and empathy.

Her focus on achieving a 1st Dan Black Belt, combined with her strong sense of self, allows Carmel to navigate life challenges for herself whilst helping others she meets on her journey to do the same. She holds a solid foundation of calming strength.

Carmel resides in Brisbane alongside her husband, who she describes as her rock and soul mate, where they raise their two sons. She is making her debut as an author as a contributor in this Extraordinary book.

Find and connect with Carmel at: www.facebook.com/profile.php?id=100087489991563&mibextid=ZbWKwL

SCARLETT, THE STORY SO FAR

L et's start at the beginning.

Our pregnancy had been a beautiful one. We had the NIPT/Harmony test at nineteen weeks. The results blew my first pregnancy with Stella (two years old) out of the water. Being older meant we didn't have to make any hard decisions, and we could finally announce our pregnancy. We didn't know the gender yet; that information was tucked nicely in a little white envelope on our dresser. We caved just before Mother's Day – and we learned we were having a baby girl, which was exactly what we wished for. I started to think of all the loveliest ways to announce our news.

At twenty-two weeks, I had a final pregnancy scan, where they measured the baby's growth. So again, all was well, and we felt blessed to be having a perfect little baby. Fast forward to three weeks later, two days after Mother's day, 2021.

I was twenty-five weeks pregnant when Stella and I were involved in a serious car accident.

As we approach the lights, another car takes the right of way, pushing us into the oncoming traffic. The impact is so severe the two vehicles were complete write-offs. It happened in the blink of an eye.

We are both screaming uncontrollably. It was the most TERRIFYING moment of my life. I kept repeating to God, 'Please let my baby be ok.'

In the emergency department, they told me that I had to be ok before they even looked at the baby. Time seemed to slow, and it made me anxious. But when they finally did the ultrasound, they told me the baby was fine. It was a frickin' miracle. I felt so lucky, and I believe my two beautiful Grandmothers were watching over us that day.

Later in the night, I was attached to a six-hour-long monitor of the baby's heartbeat, which was ok. Then for the rest of the week, I had doppler checks. Every day, it showed a solid and normal heartbeat.

In the weeks ahead, I had regular appointments with my birthing team to see how I was going, including a quick look at bub with an ultrasound to say hello. 'I will be meeting you soon,' I thought nervously.

We agreed to elect for a caesarian birth because, with my extensive injuries, there was a high risk that labour might refracture my bones. In addition, I was scared about a c-section recovery while still healing. I can't say I was excited about the newborn stage again, and I often cried in panic leading up to birth. I kept thinking, 'What is wrong with me'!? But I couldn't *shake this feeling of hardship and doom.*

Scarlett's Birth.

I was so nervous, and I was dreading what was coming. In the delivery room, while I was thinking about all the trivial worries I'd been having, everyone else was joking around about what song this baby would be born to and what the time would be. Place your bets, people.

The nurses were friendly and calming, but I cried as they cut me because I was scared that I might be able to feel it. Within a few minutes, the nurse told me, "Bub is almost out now". Then, she's out, and the nurse told me, "She's beautiful; you cooked her good." Our little Material Girl was born at 1:19 pm on a Friday. I was relieved it was over quickly, and as they lifted her over the sheet, I saw my baby girl for the first time.

Paul, my husband, was so proud; he was in love with our daughter instantly. But I could see right away that something was not right. I can acknowledge that newborns are awkward looking, but I said to Paul, "Aww, she's ugly; her head looks weird like a nublet." - which got me thinking. Paul and I laughed a little, but he was SO proud and happy. I love to see him happy. He goes with bub to be checked over and to cut the cord. The nurse kept talking to me while they stitched me up, but I knew something wasn't quite right with her head. She was making loads of noise, and they put her on a resuscitation CPAP for a bit.

Paul came back to see that I was ok; while I was still being stitched, the Paediatrician came over and said, "I'm concerned about the baby because she has a small head", and then walked away...

When the Obstetrician came over to see us, I asked her, "how small is bubs head"? She said, "Yes, a newborn baby is usually around the 35cm mark, and she measured at 30cm. So, it's quite small." Then, they take bub and Paul to recovery. I felt like the Obstetrician was nervous about it because it was a total shock to everyone in that room. No one was expecting this.

In recovery, the nurses tried getting bub to feed and do skin-to-skin. Unfortunately, bub's stats were not reading well, so they needed to monitor her closely. Eventually, they came back up and stabilised. All I could think about was what was wrong with her head. Paul was smitten, having cuddles and taking pics with his new baby girl. The Paediatrician was deciding if bub should go to neonatal care, and we eventually went to our room, but she wasn't with us long before they decided to take her down to neonatal. She stayed in Mater Mothers' NICU for the remainder of our three-week hospital stay.

Instead of snuggling our new baby and complaining about being tired, I spent the entire first night googling all about small heads in newborn babies. The first thing I discover is Microcephaly - it was very confronting. By five am, I was a mess and couldn't hold back the sobbing, and I burst into tears. Paul wakes to comfort me and asks if I'm in pain. Of course, I am, but I'm crying because I knew something was wrong with our baby. He tells me to stop googling and not to worry.

We decide to name our daughter Scarlett. A strong name for a strong baby. Stella loves this and likens her baby sister to Scarlett Overkill from the Minions movie!

We went four days of not officially knowing what was wrong. Then, over the weekend in the neonatal ward, Scarlett is tucked away in her little hot box. One of the nurses showed me some paperwork for tests requested by the Paediatrician. I instantly saw the words "Unexpected Microcephaly", and my heart sank. That was the first real confirmation of what we were facing, and I burst into tears. The nurse didn't know that I didn't know about it yet, and she tried to reassure me - but I knew better. In the coming days, bub had multiple blood tests, scans, hearing, ultrasound, renal test, and an MRI to try and paint a picture of what was happening. The Paediatrician kept mentioning genetics, but we knew it wasn't that. The days and nights were long, all rolling into one big blurry nightmare.

THE DAY OUR LIVES CHANGED FOREVER (or as we like to refer to it – Dooms Day)

It was day four. We had a family meeting in a small room with about eight or nine professionals sitting around looking at us. Paul knew it wasn't good; he was quiet.

They tell us the MRI shows - in simple terms - the trauma from the car accident caused a brain bleed, which caused severe permanent damage to her developing brain, particularly in the frontal part, with significant cerebral volume loss overall. This is why Scarlett has a small head.

Officially the diagnosis is 'Severe Unexpected Microcephaly'. And unofficially, not yet labelled with - due to her age – Spastic Quadriplegic Cerebral Palsy, all limbs affected, anywhere from a level three to five with suspected Dystonia, Hypertonia and risk of other neurological impairments. As Paul and I began to sob while we tried to process this reality, the deafening silence was overwhelming.

They told us this was something they don't usually see, as most cases are from trauma at the time of birth in a fully developed baby or caused by genetics. So, there is no clear path or answers right now. Although, they expect a high level of disability, affecting all her motor skills and cognitive abilities. It's a special case and not a typical one. We wouldn't know the severity level until she grows and starts to develop. She may never crawl, walk, run or play and may not have any functional use of all or part of her limbs. This will mean a wheelchair of sorts or frame for her. She may never be able to tell us, and we may never hear her say, "I love you, Mummy." They said her intellect would likely be severely impacted, and she would need a high level of twenty-four-hour care.

The burn of reality washed over us, and our hearts sank to the depths of the earth beneath us. *EVERYTHING* was going to be different now. All the things we had envisioned for the future with our two little girls had now been totally ripped away. We felt like our whole world was falling apart, with no control over the crumbling pieces. Finally, they left the room, and we were left alone to process what we had been told. Floods of tears poured out of us; we were gutted. The desperate feeling of wanting to wake up from this nightmare was so intense that we couldn't stop crying. The pain was indescribable. We were now grieving the loss of what was supposed to be instead of celebrating and finding joy in our newborn baby.

The 'What ifs' start to play on my mind. I felt like it was my fault, even though I knew I had no control over what had happened. But mostly, we were just heartbroken for our beautiful baby girl. Her life had been altered in the most brutal way. It was never going to be easy and never going to be – dare I say it - "normal." Stella won't be able to play with her little sister as we had hoped for her. We are older parents, and Stella will one day have to care for her little sister. - if she will. So many questions and thoughts were constantly going around in our minds. And it just felt SO unfair. The guilt was heavy.

In these early and awfully raw days, we constantly thought - WHY US? What did we do to deserve this? I started to question our beliefs. And Paul decided there was no god.

What should come naturally to a baby, such as suckling, was hard to watch. Scarlett's brain was sending signals to her body like a mixed-up puzzle. Before we left the hospital, we spent three weeks with a speech therapist working hard to teach her how to achieve this fundamental skill. The Paediatrician told us she would probably never be able to drink for herself. As I looked into her eyes, my heart fell into a million pieces because I knew the hardship that was coming for her. But I was determined to help her achieve these kinds of goals. And every time she did a little better, I praised her for doing such a great job. Together we would celebrate these small wins. If anything, during those dark times, at least, I had HOPE.

My good friend knew how much I was struggling and sourced a fantastic book for me called *Special* by Melanie Dimmitt. I can honestly say that book saved us. It validated every feeling we had; I recommend it to everyone.

Before we headed home, an obstetrician told me it was a miracle Scarlett had survived the car accident, to begin with – I suppose he was trying to help me find comfort in the fact that in car accidents as severe as ours, the placenta is, in most; if not all cases, usually rupture and the baby often dies. So I guess I found a smidge of gratitude in that statement that Scarlett's body could still grow to term despite what had happened to her in utero. But also, a lot of mixed feelings.

We decided to go home with the idea of treating Scarlett like a "normal" baby – for the first twelve months at least- to try to enjoy her and not let anything change that.

It's been a huge challenge; we each have faltered at times, but she truly is an amazing being.

Leaving the safety net of the hospital and all the professionals was a scary time. But once we were home, it was nice. However, we were only home two days before I questioned Scarlett's yellow eye colour. She was really cold, but it was winter, so I didn't think much more of it. Our doctor sent her for blood tests, and by that afternoon, she called, telling us to return to the QCH (Queensland Children's Hospital, Brisbane). We couldn't believe it. Stella was so confused.

Upon arrival, the nurses tried four different thermometers but could not get a reading of Scarlett's temperature. It was so strange. After tests, it revealed she had hyperthermia and hyponatremia. How did I not notice she was that cold? It took eight hours for her temperature to become stable again. They told us she has Diabetes Insipidus (Salt diabetes) and started a medication called Hydrochlorothiazide, which she will always need.

Whenever we think we have turned a corner, something new emerges, and the wind is knocked out of us. But I've never given up Hope. I could not tell you how often we have been admitted to the hospital or had emergency trips to the emergency department. Scarlett has had to endure more blood tests and needles in her short life than mine and Paul's whole lives combined, twice over. She has been through a lot. And I have learnt to grow a *very* thick skin in these moments. So much for acting normal in the first twelve months, right? So, I remind myself to *find the win* every day.

By November, when Scarlett was three months old, she was drinking a bottle like a champion and tolerating her meds orally, and with that, out came the Nasogastric intubation (NGT). With family, we celebrated this win and that she had proven them wrong! Finally, she was able to feed herself! Shortly after, Scarlett started Diazepam to see if it might help with the high tone in her body.

Around Christmas time, she started to roll. But the excitement was quickly overshadowed by the discovery of Infantile Spasms (also known as West Syndrome). As they increased in severity, the decline in ability took place. She stopped rolling and urgently had an EEG. The Neurologist told us to think of it like a 'bushfire', we briefly trialed

Vigabatrin, but three days later, she was put onto a more potent steroid called Prednisolone. It worked, but it was dark times in our household for ten weeks. Scarlett blew up like a balloon, accentuating her little head. Her eye swelled up, and she had rolls for days. She couldn't sleep and feeding went down the tube – literally! Hello NGT again. Sleep doesn't come easy to someone with Cerebral Palsy, and she has three meds to help her with this in the evenings, so we can both rest – This was a game changer during steroid treatment. The repeat EEG showed that the 'bushfires' had been put out. She started a preventative medication called Tegretol, which is helping for now. (We have been told she can potentially begin to wean off this medication in the coming months – fingers crossed) So, now that the Prednisolone had stopped, we could get back to normal life, right? ...No.

Two weeks later, we quickly discovered that Scarlett was having an Adrenal Crisis. This life-threatening condition occurs when there is insufficient cortisol to help heal or fight off colds and infections. This was caused by using Prednisolone. So, she went back into the hospital and onto another steroid called Hydrocortisone, though we will start to wean off this slowly once spring/summer arrives, followed by an Adrenal Gland function test. Scarlett heavily relies on medications to help her get through the day. She is on eight different kinds, some multiple times daily. Scarlett's movement pattern throws her body to a favoured side while her spine has a twist. She just started a new medication called Baclofen to assist with this. A welcomed relief to Scarlett's little body, I am sure. Soon we will get a funky second skin suit to help keep the body aligned, in conjunction with TheraTogs, which will help tame the scoliosis before it completely takes over her little body.

Funding

Navigating the NDIS world and applying for Centrelink payments has been a wild ride. We thought we would never get anywhere with it, but in time it all came. Now we can try and order equipment for Scarlett. I feel like I am pretty tough when it comes to the crunch, but every time she trials a new piece of equipment, the painting of our life starts to become clearer—quickly unveiling before our eyes. And it is, REALLY hard.

I can honestly say that every day is about survival for us. We feel like we are constantly treading water to get through. It's difficult to find joy in the hand we have been dealt. BUT... I can say that we have been showered with so much love and encouragement from near and far. Whether it's a kind word from a stranger at the shop, a nurse, from a media platform or friends and family. People have often asked me, "What can I do to help?" but sometimes, just words are enough. I find much comfort in our therapy sessions. Some therapies leave me feeling very proud and hopeful.

Scarlett just celebrated her first birthday (that was the fastest year EVER). Since birth, she has shown me how determined she is, how tolerant, how strong, and how intelligent she is.

She fought to be in this world - against the odds, to come into our lives.

Our life does not look like what he wanted, and it's difficult to come to terms with that. Grief is funny; it comes in all forms and will pop up when you least expect it. I'm not sure we will ever really come to terms with it, but my heart fills up with love when she smiles or watches Stella. And Stella (almost four years old) loves her baby sister *unconditionally*. She knows that Scarlett struggles, but she looks at her no differently than anyone else. What an empowering way to think.

With this, I welcome anyone, anywhere, to approach us to ask questions about Scarlett. I want to undo the stigma that surrounds people with disabilities. I won't bite you 😊 please come and chat with me.

I want to share her story and bring awareness to her situation and the challenges she faces. It is my own form of mental health therapy too. I want to connect with people to share the joys and the hard times with anyone willing to listen. Some people have said that she was meant to be here for a reason - maybe to teach and guide others about this life. So, while we learn - we share and grow together.

We can't 'fix' Scarlett, but we will do EVERYTHING we can to give her the BEST chance in life to do anything. We will celebrate her wins, lift her up, and advocate for her. We will love her, and we will protect her with everything in us.

She is our little fighter.

Our little miracle.

Our little Scarlett Overkill

CHRISTINE MCTIGHE

Christine is a typical Piscean. Lover of music, dance and art; daydreamer. She wears her heart on her sleeve, often putting others before herself. At forty years old she is a married, mother of two young girls (three and one) and a Furr baby (nine); who has worked in child-care for twenty-one years.

Having always been a nurturer, she was inspired to care for children after her first niece was born in 2001. She is kind and passionate about child safety. Christine has successfully ran week long campaigns through her workplace – raising funds and bringing awareness to the importance of a child's voice, and how to stay safe; to children, their families and the community.

She is a supporter of Act for Kids, Bravehearts and Daniel Morcombe Foundation. She firmly believes that child protection is everyone's business.

Christine is now a full-time carer for her youngest daughter Scarlett, who has Microcephaly and Spastic Quadriplegic Cerebral Palsy. And her new endeavour is to bring about awareness of disability, to shine a positive light on and remove the stigma that surrounds it. To show people not to be afraid. She does this by sharing the highs and lows of Scarlett's journey, knowing that even if it helps just one other parent going through a similar situation–which in turn, also helps Christine heal. Hoping to inspire others, to embrace disability and be brave in approaching people that seem - a little or *a lot* different.

You can follow Christine and Scarlett's story on Instagram at:
www.instagram.com/scarlett_overkill2021

AN UNEXPECTED MIRACLE

K nowing someone's story is to know their strength. Knowing invites change. With change, one's potential is infinite.

I woke up in a hospital bed to the poking of my belly. The doctor was talking to my mom while lifting my shirt and feeling my stomach. I hated being touched, especially my belly. It made my skin crawl. And to top it off, I was wearing white undies. "Were they see-through? Of all days to wear white undies, why today?" I thought. "This is the worst day of my life."

I was embarrassed, I felt miserable and violated.

I just wanted to be home in my own bed…and wondered, Is this just a bad dream? It had been a whirlwind night, and I was living a bad dream. My mom had taken me to the after-hours clinic the previous evening because her motherly instincts were peaked. She explained to the physician's assistant that I just didn't seem right. I wasn't acting like myself. Usually, I was active, loved playing competitive soccer and tennis and enjoyed going to practices. However, the past day or so, I was tired, refused to go to practice, my skin was more pale than usual, and my coordination seemed a tad off in my soccer game the previous day.

I was a tired, fit, brown curly-haired teenage girl with six small bruises on my legs, two of which were across my shins from being slide-tackled in soccer the day before. To the doctor, there was nothing of genuine concern.

After some inquiry about my life, the physician's assistant believed that I was just tired. I had a full load of honors classes in my freshman year of high school, played competitive soccer, and varsity tennis and had just made it onto the varsity soccer team. "Teens just need more rest," he insisted, "but we can draw some blood just to be safe."

I had the blood tests, and we waited. I figured it was nothing and would be sent home soon.

Thirty minutes later, the physician's assistant seemed concerned as he peeked his head into our room and told us to wait for the doctor to arrive. My platelets were really low, but that's all we knew.

Now we waited and waited with trepidation. Something must be wrong if the doctor was coming to see us. Fear of the unknown felt heavier than I could bear. The doctor finally arrived. He entered the room quietly with a concerned demeanour. He explained that my platelet count was very low and is typically only this low when someone is receiving chemotherapy. Platelets are responsible for blood clotting, so I was at extreme risk for bleeding, and any trauma to my head or belly could be life-threatening. He instructed us to go immediately to the Children's Hospital for further testing and treatment.

We arrived at the hospital around midnight, and they escorted me to my room. After checking in, I finally fell asleep, a brief break from my new unwelcome reality. Now Dr O, the Hematologist or blood specialist, explained to my mom that I most likely had Idiopathic Thrombocytopenic Purpura (ITP). A condition where my immune system attacked my platelets, but all my other blood cells and lab values were normal. Treatment would consist of two days of IV medication, regular monitoring and a somewhat unknown future. When my platelet count increased and was in a safer range, I would be allowed to go home. ITP can either correct itself quickly, or become chronic, and each patient responds differently to treatment. However, because of puberty and hormones, it can be hard to treat in teenage girls. My life wasn't in imminent danger as long as I kept myself safe and away from soccer and contact sports. Yet, life without soccer felt like a death in itself. How could I give up everything that I loved? I felt so distraught and confused.

The doctor supposed a possible cause, that I was burning the candle at both ends with all my activities. I couldn't believe what I heard, but I may have been pushing my body to the limits. I played through a cold during soccer tryouts and was running on very little sleep. How could this be? I felt terrible. I was scared. And now I wouldn't be able to play sports...My world was crumbling!

I was mad... It felt like my life was over.

"Let's get this treatment started, so I can get out of here," I thought. The medication infusion began, and it made me shiver and ache. My head throbbed. I tried to pass the time by playing Scrabble with my mom, doing homework, and sleeping. I'd gaze past the empty bed next to mine out the window and think of how alone I felt.

I missed my soccer game. Yet, little did I know; something was about to happen that would change my life forever. Something painful and beautiful that would later awaken me to part of my purpose in this life.

The next day while in the depths of despair, a new roommate joined me. The nurse pulled back the white and blue checkered curtain, and brought in a young couple with a small, bald, chubby-cheeked girl. She was asleep in her dad's arms and appeared very sick. She was only three or four years old.

The nurses and doctors worked quickly to check her in. They hooked her up to a plethora of pumps and tubes. I could sense their worry, and it scared me. She interacted very little, and the mood in the room was very sombre. I overheard the doctors and nurses say they didn't think she would live through the night. Here I was, fourteen years old, sharing the room for the night with a little girl who could die at any time. I was afraid. I didn't know what to expect. Her worried parents clung to each other and kept praying and hoping for the best. She stayed asleep most of the time. The pumps beeped frequently, and the nurses were in-and-out to care for her. Occasionally her mom would make small talk with my mom and me. She was very open and kind. She explained that her sweet Ashley was born with neutropenia, a condition where she doesn't have enough white blood cells in her blood to fight infections. And on top of that, she was diagnosed with a very rare form of leukemia or blood cancer that only a few other people in the world were reported to have. She had undergone countless procedures and treatments and recently received a bone marrow transplant. Unfortunately, she was having some complications from the transplant, and her immune system was still not very strong at fighting infections. Her little body was tired and frail. I watched with fear and prayed silently for her. Somehow, I found myself thinking more of her than myself. I had just received life-altering news, but her life had barely begun and now could be ending. She had been fighting her whole life, enduring many painful and scary treatments, and her future was uncertain. My illness and struggle now seemed so small.

The morning sunlight shone through the window, and I awoke to a squeaky, high-pitched voice demanding breakfast. Much to all our surprise, it was Ashley. She made it through the night. But what I heard her say next made me realise that her living through the night wasn't just a mere coincidence. It was a miracle.

"Mommy!' she said," Jesus came to see me last night, and we talked."

"Really?" her mom asked.

"He came to take me home, but I asked him if I could stay because mommy and daddy still needed me. So he said I could stay this time, but next time I would need to go."

She was so happy to be there with her mom. Despite being so sick, she never complained. She spoke her mind, knew what she wanted, gently teased the nurses, and loved with her whole heart. She really impressed me. I marvelled at her strength and courage and her will to live. She was a fighter. She was so sick, yet she never let her illness consume her. Amidst her suffering, she was thinking of those she loved.

My fourteen-year-old self was not excited initially to be rooming with a three or four-year-old little girl. But the cosmos had aligned, and I was gifted this special meeting with Ashley.

My treatment continued till midday, and then my doctors finally allowed me to go home. But, to my dismay, my sporting career was over, and I was under strict orders to rest and avoid being hit in the head or abdomen. I still didn't feel great, but I was thrilled to go home. I don't think I fully understood it then, but I was so intrigued by Ashley and her example. I realised that my problems were minuscule in comparison to hers. And no matter how much I loved sports, that life and relationships are truly a gift. It was hard to feel sorry for myself when I saw what she was going through. Then, my perspective on life and what is truly important started shifting.

A few close friends visited and kept me company when I returned home, but I still felt alone and unsure how to navigate this new reality. When times were hard, I thought of Ashley.

When I didn't feel good, I thought of Ashley.

When I was making up the schoolwork I missed, I thought about Ashley. I even wrote a poem about her. On days I felt good, I would take Ashley small gifts in the hospital.

Life was weird after being plunged into the medical world. I missed sports. I struggled to keep up with my school assignments, and I believed receiving good grades was all I had left. I barely had the energy to get through the day, let alone have energy for friends or high school football games or dances. Lab draws and doctor visits were frequent, and each excursion zapped me. My hope for a quick resolution of ITP didn't happen. Another hospitalisation, more treatment changes and new side effects from the drugs were now somewhat routine. I was put on steroids which increased my appetite, made me retain fluids, especially when I ate salty food, and I gained twenty pounds in the first two to three weeks. My cheeks were now chubby like Ashley's and covered in acne. I felt awful on the drugs, and they didn't enhance my physical performance, like in the movies. I had massive mood swings and went from happy and peaceful to furious and raging in less than two seconds. The drugs were worse than the illness. Typically, people with ITP are prone to bleeding issues, but I was fortunate not to have those issues. My primary manifestation of the disease was that I would bruise very easily, which in many cases was more alarming to those around me and a constant reminder that something wasn't quite right inside me. Being covered in dozens of bruises reminded me of my brokenness and imperfections. Again, when it felt too heavy...I would think of Ashley.

Dr O and the nurses Debbie and Dorothy became like family. I would see them at least once to twice weekly. They truly cared about me and took an interest in what I was doing. They somehow made being sick seem not so bad. They made unpleasant pokes fun, listened to my concerns, helped me with my science projects for school, and even challenged me to research vitamins and supplements to help certain conditions. They showed me that life doesn't stop because of an illness. We are still capable, able to thrive and make a difference. Watching and learning from them made me want to follow in their footsteps. I wanted to make a difference for kids like Ashley and myself.

Interacting with Ashley and other kids like her was rewarding. It's as if time stood still in their presence, and each moment was precious. I savoured and celebrated the little things. I could relate in some small way to what they were going through, and we rallied together to support each other. The culture was inclusive. We felt the highest of highs and weathered the lowest of lows together. Though the atmosphere was typically upbeat and cheerful, the world of cancer and blood disorders didn't come without sadness. Sometimes even after the most courageous fight, the strongest fighters succumbed to illness and emerged with their well-deserved angel wings.

Ashley was my first friend to walk me down this path. She fought hard for about another year before she died peacefully in her parents' arms. At the funeral, her dad recounted that first night we shared a room in the hospital when they didn't know if she'd survive the night. Where Jesus came for Ashley, and she asked to stay because her mom and dad needed her. Jesus agreed that she could stay that time, but she'd have to go next time. She was worried about her parents and taking care of those she loved in her trials and suffering. In the week leading up to Ashley's death, she slept a lot. She woke up the day before she died and was pretty alert for a short time. Her dad took this time to talk with her. He said he loved her and knew it was almost time for her to go home. He told her it was okay for her to go. She had fought valiantly and completed her mission. He assured her that Mommy and Daddy would miss her but would be okay. In her quick-witted, squeaky-pitched voice, she matter-of-factly told her dad that he better be good so he could return to Jesus, or she'll come to flick him on the ear to remind him.

As he shared, I could imagine the scene and hear her voice resonating in my head. I laughed because it was typical of who she was. I was still overcome with sadness by her passing, but my heart was comforted to know that she was no longer suffering and looking down on those she loved. I felt humbled and grateful that I got to know and learn from her, and I wondered how her parents could go on without her. I wished I could do more to offer comfort. Time continued to pass, and the treatments I had been taking were no longer effective. I opted to stop all medications because of the side effects and try holistic remedies, dietary modifications, and lifestyle changes to support my physical health. Under the care of an integrative health practitioner who was also a medical doctor, I began to find healing.

My energy increased. My platelet count started to increase slowly, and I was clear to play tennis again. Each year my platelet count was a little higher. Before I graduated at seventeen, my platelet count had stabilised close to the normal range.

The healing continued during college. My heart led me to obtain my bachelor's degree in nursing, and I was hired fresh out of college at Children's Hospital of San Diego in the hematology/oncology department. For fifteen years, I rubbed shoulders with and ministered to many kids and families like Ashley's. I tried to emulate the examples of Dr O and my amazing nurses, Debbie and Dorothy. Those families, and my amazing co-workers, shared in all the milestones of my life and claimed a special place in my heart. They watched me grow, get married, start and grow my family.

An unexpected, uncomfortable, and undesirable couple of nights in the hospital all those years ago, followed by a journey to healing, has become one of my most cherished blessings. That sacred and special night with Ashley with heavenly and earthly angels implanted a grandeur view of what this life is truly about. It served as a catalyst to help me understand my life's purpose and the divine gifts I have to offer.

I truly believe that before we came to this earth, we were spirits and had formed relationships like we experience today. I'm sure that Ashley and I made a contract to meet at that exact time to inspire and guide me when I desperately needed hope, understanding, and perspective. I witnessed her light, love and joy, which has helped me develop that same love, light and joy to share with others.

There are no coincidences. There is a divinity within each of us, and each of us have a special part to play in the divine master plan. Recently, I welcomed my seventth child, sweet baby Ruby, into the world. She had some genetic abnormalities and was born without breath at thirty-one weeks.

I never dreamed that this would be my reality, that I would be the mother of an angel. But Ruby, like Ashley, has been a great teacher and gift in my life. Each experience and lesson I have learned has prepared me for this season of my life and invites me to grow. I've been a friend. I've been a patient. I've been the nurse. I've been the parent of a sick and struggling child. I've been the coach supporting other parents, and now I am the mother who lost her baby and is on the receiving end of ministering angels.

In my trials, I am reminded that knowing someone beyond the superficial invites change. So, I pray that even in this new life experience I have been asked to endure, and other trials of life that may come my way and yours, we may notice the gifts and change around us and be that change for others.

GINA COOPER

Gina is a consummate professional who embodies ease and grace in her soul, which is felt by all who experience her.

Gina is a wife, mother, nurse, coach, and child advocate. She lives in Nashville, TN with her amazing husband and kids. She has seven children – three girls and three boys Earthside and one beautiful daughter Ruby in Heaven.

Her many years caring for hundreds of children going through cancer and other life-altering diseases plus her experiences with her own children with unique struggles has given her a profound awareness of the grief and loss. Gina's own loss of newborn Ruby has personalised what so many go through and has been a catalyst for helping others to have a healthy physical, emotional, and spiritual life.

Gina enjoys an active lifestyle, and loves spending time with her family, playing tennis, gardening, and baking. Her purpose is to support others on their healing journey, combining with her medical knowledge with her favourite natural solutions and her keen insight on how the body, mind, and emotions work together. Her compassion and love for others and her Heavenly father and daughter are her guiding lights.

Find Gina here:
https://www.facebook.com/gina.cooper.3511
ginacooper@gmail.com

TURNING PAIN INTO PURPOSE

I looked down at the stick. You know, THE stick. The pregnancy stick. I kept telling myself, "There is no way that I could be pregnant!" I hadn't been pregnant for over nine years and was already in my forties. I already had a 13-year-old son and a -ten-year-old daughter. How can this happen?

For some reason, I sensed I was pregnant. My body felt different; it was that mother's intuition. Serendipitously, I had two pregnancy tests in my bathroom cabinet. I took one test and waited 10 minutes, which felt like an eternity. When I saw the two lines, I couldn't believe my eyes, so I took the second test. And you guessed it. It was positive too! My heart began beating, and fear overcame me. How was I going to tell my husband? How will the kids respond? And the questions went on and on in my mind.

My husband was lying in bed, and I brought the two tests to him. He looked at me and said, "What is this?" I guess he had forgotten what a pregnancy test looked like, I said, "It's a pregnancy test, and it's saying I am pregnant!" He looked at me in shock. He felt the same as I did. I quickly went to our local store to get a better test because those Dollar Tree cheap tests have to be defective, right? Nope, that test told me the same thing. I was pregnant. We were having a baby. I sat in my bathroom, all I wanted to do was cry, but all I could do was laugh because I was in utter shock. Fast forward to a couple of months later, we had accepted the pregnancy and told our family, and they were very excited to welcome another beautiful baby.

Having another baby wasn't in our plans, but God had a beautiful plan that would change our lives forever in ways we never could've imagined. When you are a woman in your forties, the doctors already see you as a high risk. The doctors want you to take every test and watch to ensure there are no abnormalities in the pregnancy. When I was pregnant with my last two children, I always opted out of any test that would tell if your baby was Down syndrome or not because it wouldn't change the fact of having the baby or not, and this pregnancy was not different. They asked me numerous times if I wanted to take the test, and I would tell them no several times. Some women would like to know, and be prepared, but I wanted to enjoy this pregnancy, and for me, it would just be added stress.

At twenty weeks, most doctors will have you do a comprehensive ultrasound, so that is what we did. I am always trying to read the sonographer's face because they really can't tell you if anything is wrong. When he said, "I will be right back", my husband and I started to panic. We wondered what could be wrong. The radiologist came in and told us that our baby had extra skin on his neck and that there was a 99% chance that our baby would be born with Down syndrome. At that moment, I felt like all the air went out of the room. The doctor told us we could opt to have an amniocentesis test to know for sure if our baby had Down syndrome or not. They asked if we wanted to terminate our baby, and at that point I said, please don't ever ask me again. We opted out of all the tests or terminating our baby and said, "we are going to trust God, and he will give us the baby that he wants us to have."

A couple months went by, and the doctors wanted to do another ultrasound. During this test, they found a heart defect called ASD, and our baby would need open heart surgery at about six months of age. Our hearts sank again, and I thought, how am I going to deal -   with not only Down syndrome, but my baby having open heart surgery? It all felt like such a heavy load to carry, and all I could do was cry and ask God to heal my baby. We asked our family and our church to pray. We prayed that God would give us a healthy baby boy.

The Doctors asked us to meet with genetic counsellors, to prepare us for life with a baby with Down syndrome, and they talked us through his heart defect as well. It was a lot to take in but I chose to only tell our Pastor at the time and asked him to pray. We trusted that God would take care of our son.

Our son was born on October 3rd, 2021, a month earlier than we expected. He weighed just 5lbs 4oz. So, the nurses took him immediately to the NICU with my husband, where he stayed for the next week. He was born during the end of Covid so only my husband and I could go and see him in the NICU. No one else, not even my kids, were able to visit him. Nothing was said about a Down syndrome diagnosis for our son, so we thought maybe he didn't have it, maybe the doctors were wrong.

We spent the next couple of days loving and getting to know our son. We admired his little fingers, his cute toes and his dark, beautiful eyes. To us, he was our son who was born healthy and that is all that mattered. My husband and I could not agree on a name before he was born. Our other two children's names came right away, but this time around, it was much harder. We wanted the perfect name for him, but nothing seemed to stick.

A couple of days went by, and the doctors confirmed that our son was diagnosed with Down syndrome. My husband and I just cried. Sometimes I felt bad for crying because I didn't want it to mean that I loved my son any less. A friend of mine, whose daughter has Down syndrome said to me, "Let yourself feel every emotion, even the bad ones." So that's what I did. I began to feel so many different emotions. Feelings of joy quickly turned into fear. Feelings of loss for what you thought would be. I wondered if my son would be able to have the same opportunities as all the other kids. What would his life look like, and would I be able to handle it all? It felt so heavy at times, but I firmly believe that our son was not a mistake, and he was put on this Earth for a purpose.

As my husband and I were processing everything we realised that we still needed to give our son a name. When I was in my room the name Levi came to me. The name Levi means, "harmony and to come together." As soon as we knew the meaning of Levi, my husband and I said, "that is his name."

We hope that Levi will unite and bring people together like never before. Our hope is that his life will be used as a light for so many. He has already done that in so many ways.

When Levi was in the NICU, he was blessed with amazing nurses. I will never forget one nurse named Nancy. She helped me so much as I navigated through everything. There were moments when I would be holding Levi, crying, and she would put her hand on my shoulder and tell me everything was going to be ok. She was always there to offer a smile or talk with me when I needed someone to listen. I will never forget when she looked at me and said, "Thank you for giving Levi a chance." She said, "I know that this is not the norm, but you have given him a chance at life, and I want to say thank you." Her words of encouragement meant so much, then and now.

It was time for Levi to go home, and I wanted to go and thank all the nurses. Nancy was there, and before we left, she said, "I made something special for Levi." She handed me a bracelet that she had made for him. It was in the colour of his birthstone. When she gave it to me, she looked at me and said, "Do not lose your joy." I have never forgotten those words. She said, "remember the joy that Levi is going to bring into your lives." She was truly a God send.

The entire family was so excited to meet Levi for the first time, but I was so nervous. How was I going to tell my family? When would be the right time to tell the children? There were so many unanswered questions, and I was trying my hardest to enjoy each moment. I don't know why I was so afraid to tell my family and friends because I knew they would fall in love with Levi as soon as they saw him. We let about a month pass before we told our older children. I told my husband,

Kurt, that I thought we should tell them about Levi's diagnosis because I didn't want them to hear it from someone else. At this point, we had told most of our immediate family.

I'll never forget the night. We sat our kids down and said, "we need to talk with you." Of course, they became nervous and wondered what we were about to say. We looked at them and said, "We know that you love Levi very much, but there is something we need to tell you. Levi was born with Down syndrome." My daughter Charlotte had some questions about the diagnosis and asked what it was. My husband's uncle had Down syndrome, so they had a little understanding of what it was. My son Peyton was very quiet, he is a processor. I could tell that he was thinking. I said, "Peyton, it's ok if you have questions or if you feel a little uncertain. I felt the same way." He just looked at me and smiled. Then my daughter said, "this makes me love Levi even more, I will always be there to protect and love him." We all had a good cry and gave Levi a million kisses.

Levi is almost one year old now, and it's been so amazing to watch the special relationship he has with his brother and sister. They love him so much, and I know that Levi's life has taught them a lot. I am so grateful for the bond they have.

We had a couple of months to enjoy Levi before his open-heart surgery. I am here to tell you that nothing prepares you to see your child endure so much pain. I had talked to other parents who had experienced the same thing, but when it's your child, it is so difficult.

April 21st is a day that I will never forget. It was the day of Levi's surgery. He was on the operating table for over six 6 hours to fix his little heart. We went in early that morning so the doctors could prepare him for surgery. Then the moment came to take him in for his surgery. The nurse came and said, "give your baby a kiss, and you will see him in a few hours." She took him from my arms, and then my husband and I just held each other and cried as she walked down the hall. It was the longest six hours of our lives. The nurse would come and give us an update every hour or so. She would say, "ok, he is on the bypass now. They are operating on him, and now they are closing him up." It was such a blessing to have that update from her, so we weren't just sitting there in the dark.

Then the moment came, and the surgeon came out. Dr C told us that everything went perfectly. They repaired what they needed to, and now Levi was on his way to recovery. Dr C was a fantastic surgeon, and he talked us through every detail. He was patient, and I was amazed at what they could do. I will always be thankful to God for using him to make Levi's heart the way it should be.

I spent the next seven days at Children's Hospital Orange County with Levi. I slept in the room with him. I saw him experience moments of pain where I couldn't do anything but try and comfort him, and moments of feeling so hopeless. There was a day that was really difficult. The nurses were trying to get Levi as comfortable as they could, but he was having a hard time. I cried out to God and asked him to please help my son and give him some relief. Have you ever felt that way? Like there was never going to be an end to your pain. That is how I felt. I asked God to please help him. I left his room for a moment and went to a room they had for the parents. In this room was a journal of parents who had been there before. I began to read the stories of so many families who had been through exactly what I was going through. It was at THAT moment that I felt God say, "It's going to be ok. I am taking care of Levi."

Sometimes we need to feel it in our spirit and hear it for ourselves, and that's precisely what had happened in that moment.

Levi had some hard days, but today, and he is doing fantastic. His heart is working as it should, and he is getting stronger every day. Before his heart surgery, he was only in the fifthth percentile for growth, and now he is at the 75th percentile. We are so thankful that he is doing so well, and so grateful to all the doctors and nurses who cared for him during that time. We can never thank them enough.

This past year of Levi's life has been filled with so many highs and lows. There were days I felt like I couldn't do it all. All the appointments, all the therapy sessions, all the sleepless nights. I would ask God, "Are you sure you picked the right Mom?"

Have you ever felt like that? Like you're in a hopeless situation or that you didn't have all the answers? Me too. I've sometimes felt like I couldn't even catch my breath, but I am amazed at how God has helped me every step of the way. He has given me the strength I needed when I felt like I couldn't move forward. He has given me the courage to advocate for Levi to ensure he has all he needs. He has used the pain that I've been through to bring a new passion into my life. He has given me a new joy through Levi's life that I never knew was possible.

We will all encounter difficult times in our lives, but I am here to tell you – don't give up. There is a God who loves you, values you and has a purpose in everything in your life. Nothing is by accident. Where God has you is exactly where He wants you to be, and if you trust in Him, He will guide you every step of the way.

Three things that have help me in the challenging moments:

1. Having quiet time: it's my time to talk with God, take a walk or have some time for me. Sometimes it's only five minutes and sometimes it's an hour, but I always try to find the time because it's that important.
2. Connect with others: Don't do life alone. I've connected with amazing Moms and Dads who have kids with Down syndrome or special needs, and it's been so beautiful to talk through even the smallest details about Levi's life. They have been there to pray with me, talk with me or answer any questions I may have. I know it can be hard to step out to meet with people, but we are so much better together than we are alone.
3. Realise there is purpose in your pain: I firmly believe there are no accidents. Everything that happens in our life has purpose. Levi's life is for a reason, and I know that God is going to use his life to touch so many. Process your pain but don't stay there. Your story matters, and your story will be used to help those around you.

Though having Levi was not in our plans, my family always say we could not imagine our lives without him. He has brought us so much joy, and he has taught us so much about ourselves. He has taught us how to love with no conditions. He has taught us that there is beauty in the imperfections, and he has led us to have fun along the journey. Thank you, God, for entrusting me, and my family with Levi. He has been one of the biggest blessings in my life, and I am honoured to be his Mom.

I can't wait to see all that God has in store for this mighty, strong, world shaker, Levi Anthony Simon!

HERMELINDA SIMON

Hermelinda Simon is a mother, speaker, mentor and believes that everyone has a story. She believes that your story matters and can be used in a powerful way.

She desires to bring hope, joy and love and to remind you that you are not alone. She prays that her life story can inspire and bring encouragement to others in their darkest hours.

She has been in full-time children's and family ministry for over 25 years and desires for every family and child to know that they are loved and have a God-given purpose.

Hermelinda lives in California with her amazing husband Kurt and their three wonderful children.

Follow Hermelinda, where she shares her journey on www.insta gram.com/Luvlevi5

CHERISHING A LIFE OUTSIDE OF THE BOX

I recently read that when we give hope to others, we derive pleasure that is as strong as when we receive hope.

I know what it's like to feel truly hopeless;

But If I told you I changed it all by tapping on my face and saying some words, you'd probably think I was crazy.

It's uncomfortable to remember how unwell I was. The constant onslaught of thoughts, the what ifs, the shoulds, my head felt like a Monday morning New York traffic jam full of angry drivers that missed their breakfast coffee. My chest felt as if it had been overtaken by butterflies, that they were all frantically trying to escape with nowhere to get out. I'd break a sweat sitting, and my insides and hands felt like they constantly trembled. I always felt breathless. I felt like this for years…

Forever promising myself if I wasn't feeling any better soon, I would seek help. This went on for so long and the thought of making an appointment to seek a mental health plan filled me with fear. I'd had GP's offer scripts for medications that suggested I could get worse before feeling better and the thought of getting worse… was scary, so much scarier than the normal amount of fear that my anxiety would have racing through my body.

It would paralyse me.

What did I have to be depressed or anxious about?

Everything around me was wonderful. I was a new mum to two beautiful kids, had a new house, and had just married my best friend, yet my mind had spiralled.

The low I felt trapped in felt familiar but had gone away in the past, and I thought this would too. I'd experienced depression when I was younger, however, the autonomy and independence adult life gave me served me, and it had mostly given me a break from feeling so empty.

No one warns you of the strength that is needed to become a Mum. Pregnancy and giving birth are only the first tests. No one tells you that you're going to birth what will become your greatest teacher, and all that was left unhealed will be stirred within.

It was years before I sought help, and the traditional therapy left me angry, and I struggled to see the point. So, when looking for more, I turned to Google, as most of us do at some point, trying to find alternative anxiety treatments. I clicked through the suggestions and found a YouTube video with a guy on stage talking about EFT Tapping and as he tapped his face the crowd copied. I thought he was crazy, but at that point, I was willing to give anything a go.

In the first round I really thought it or I was crazy, but I continued.

Top of the head

Eyebrow

Beside the eye

Under the eye

Under the nose

Chin

Collarbone

Under the arm

and again,

and again,

And it wasn't long before I felt a wave of calm wash over my body.

A feeling I hadn't felt in so long. I felt calm, perhaps for the first time since my childhood.

I knew that moment was significant. But I don't think I will ever find the words that will convey just how much that moment was the start of what would change my life.

I was holding onto a lot. I knew I had trauma that needed some work, and my Neurodivergent mind only fuelled my situation. Since my ADHD diagnosis, so much makes sense. I'm so easily triggered, and I hold onto and ruminate on what many may think insignificant. My body likes to keep the score.

I've let go of the emotional attachments or wounds left by life experiences, childhood traumas, and so many comments along the way that have made my heart sting. Tapping changed so much for me that I felt called to learn how I could teach it to others in a way that would enable them to change their life too.

It has supported me and my mental health through my healing journey. It's allowed me emotional space and strength as a Mum that I didn't know I had in me. I am a Mum to two incredible children. "The pigeon pair" and Tapping supported me through the diagnosis process of my Son and Daughter, who are ASD/PDA and ADHD and with that comes as much magic as there are challenges.

Society, and the world seems to make it feel like everything has to fit into a box. If you don't fit that box or their mould, then you are wrong, and you have to learn to fit in. But fitting in can be traumatic. I know because I watched my son dim his sparkle to fit in, and it triggered a spiral in him that resembled the one I'd experienced myself. He lost his sense of self, his inner sense of safety, and anything outside our four walls would feel like a threat.

Then there are those like my daughter who yearns to fit in but having such a sensitive heart can make navigating friendships tricky. She craves to be understood and accepted by her peers but fitting in is exhausting and depletes her.

It can feel like there is always a battle when you're a Neurodivergent Mum. The fight in itself can be draining when coming up against a system so broken.

It takes the kind of bravery and strength I didn't think I had.

I was white knuckling my days before mum life!

There has been so much learning and just as much unlearning, and I'll forever be relearning and surrendering. While trying to learn as much as I could about Neurodivergent minds to support my kids, I realised they were a mirror of me, and perhaps my struggles with Anxiety and Depression were contributed to by undiagnosed ADHD within me. I was pretty positive; it all started to make sense to me, the Teacher comments at school, the emotional outbursts, the coping strategies I'd acquired to gain some sense of control.

When seeking a referral for my diagnosis, I was again told antidepressants, and SSRI would be my best option. My refusal to those was noted on my referral with a big question mark over ADHD.

I was right. I am ADHD.

Everything happens for a reason.

I can't expect you to understand how Tapping has helped me get through some of my darkest moments and helped me transform the lives of others without offering you a chance to give it ago.

So, get weird with me.

Start tapping on these points with whatever hand feels comfortable to you.

The side of the hand, tapping the part you'd use to karate chop something

The top of the head

The eyebrow point just above where your eyebrow starts

Beside your eye

Under your eye

Under your nose, above your lip

Chin

Collarbone – the spot just under the bone

Underarm – if you were to wear a bra, where the band would sit.

Before you begin, I invite you to take a deep breath through the nose and slowly out your mouth as you check in with how you're feeling.

With the current state of the world and whatever has pulled you to read this book, I'm going to assume that overwhelm is a familiar state of being for you, and I invite you to use this example.

Side of the hand-

Even though I feel overwhelmed, I choose to love and accept myself anyway. Even though I feel overwhelmed, I choose to love and accept myself regardless. Even though I feel overwhelmed, I choose to love and accept myself.

Top of the head- This overwhelm

Eyebrow- This overwhelm I am feeling

Beside the eye- I just feel so completely overwhelmed

Under the eye- I'm just so overwhelmed

Under the nose- So overwhelmed

Chin- Just so overwhelmed

Collarbone- There's just so much to do

Under arm- There's so much to think

Top of the head- It's just so overwhelming

Eyebrow- I feel so overwhelmed

Beside the eye- This overwhelm is consuming me

Under the eye- I just feel so overwhelmed

Under the nose- So overwhelmed

Chin- All of this overwhelm

Collarbone- This overwhelm I am feeling

Underarm- This overwhelm that isn't serving me

Top of the head- This overwhelm is exhausting

Eyebrow point- I give myself permission

Beside the eye- To let this overwhelm go

Under the eye- To release the feeling of overwhelm

Under the nose- I let this overwhelm go

Chin- I release this overwhelm

Collarbone - I am releasing all of this overwhelm I've been feeling

Underarm- I am letting this overwhelm go

Top of the head- Letting go of all the pressure this overwhelm has been creating

Eyebrow - Just letting it go
Beside the eye- Letting go of what isn't serving me
Under the nose- I am letting it go
Chin- I am letting it all go
Collarbone- Releasing all of this overwhelm
Underarm- I can be free of this overwhelm
Once you have felt the intensity of the feeling you are releasing dissolve, I'd like to encourage you to fill the emotional space you've created with emotions you want to embrace.
Top of the head- I am Me
Eyebrow point- I am Calm
Beside the eye- I am present
Under the eye- I am grounded
Under the nose- I am capable
Chin- I am enough
Collarbone- I am Worthy
Underarm- I am loved
Top of the head- I am supported
Eyebrow- I am divinely guided
Beside the eye- I am aligned
Under the eye- I am me
Under the nose - I am incredible
Chin- I am here for a reason

I like to finish with a deep breath on the Collarbone point with - And

I choose to love and accept myself.

When I first started, it felt like magic. I would tap through the most random of triggers, and I was able to calm my nervous system in the moment. Then as I let go of my stories and the emotional wounds I'd been holding on to for too long, I felt like I was being opened up to more and more experiences that would allow me to see just how potent this crazy-sounding modality can be.

I started sharing tips on Instagram, and as I became certified, the world was closing its doors because of the global pandemic. So, to overcome the discomfort of feeling helpless, I did all I knew, and I showed up

LIVE and tapped with viewers on whatever they were struggling with, wherever they were in the world. They showed up daily to my LIVES to watch as we released the fear, frustration and helplessness together as the world went into lockdown.

I feel blessed to have introduced Tapping to groups of Autistic children. To my amazement, these kids who were buzzing, stimming and flapping in their seats, changed within moments. Simply by following along, using words very similar to what you've just used, the noises eased, the flapping stopped, and the group calmed. So amazed, the kids started suggesting all the different moments they struggle with, where this Tapping would be useful to them.

I've worked with tired, burnt-out Mums, guiding them to let go of the emotional wounds of unspoken moments. I helped them release emotions that burdened them, so they could find more ease and peace in their present life.

One of my clients was a a teenager with an alphabet soup of diagnoses, who came to me so anxious the thought of their Mum leaving their side was too much to bare. After we worked together, I watched them conquer shopping centres on their own, and we created ease so they could release the internal sensations that were provoked within them. They went from the feeling of repulsion at the thought of touching cardboard, to receiving photos of them carrying cardboard pizza boxes.

I hold space for my clients as they revisit some of their darkest moments, allowing them to feel safe to feel their pain. Often holding back a tear myself as they truly start to feel free of the trauma that had weighed on them since childhood.

When I say I changed my life by tapping on my face and saying some words, I am not lying.

It has allowed me to release my anxieties enough to hear and trust my intuition again, and it's given me the strength to be brave enough to break cycles that don't serve me and that don't serve my children. It's given me the confidence to embrace not fitting in a box and to show my kids that being different is something to be cherished and cele-brated; it doesn't mean we are less than others.

It's offered patience, to allow my children the space to explore, do things their way, and be there to support them when needed. It's encouraged us to trust our inner knowing and to value and prioritise what feels good to us.

Through supporting my son in his recovery journey, we have had to distance ourselves from systems that weren't serving us. I've been able to release all the fear and frustrations surrounding those expectations that were crippling to him. As we navigate our unschooling journey, I hope to be able to support my kids to live a life they can love, to inspire them and allow them to feel safe and valued in the world and to support them through their challenges. So, I release the pressure of the shoulds as they arise and make space for me to trust that doing things differently will serve us long term.

I feel like Tapping has become my superpower, and I love that I now get to share my journey and the magic of Tapping with the world.

JESS MUNKS

Jess is a Neurospicy Mumma with two ASD/ADHD children, who has combined her unique life experience, strong passion for supporting better mental well-being and the power of EFT Tapping.

EFT is so incredibly versatile in its ability to help create ease in your world, Jess uses it alongside other tools and strategies to help support parents and children, no matter their Neurotype, to create a life where they're able to embrace more calm and emotional regulation.

She works from a space of releasing the emotional attachments to life experiences or trauma, in turn reducing and managing physical pain.

Guiding her clients through letting go of the stories that create the core beliefs that keep them stuck, Jess is the living proof that using EFT can change your life, and it shows in the way she works and shares her journey in her community.

With clients all over the globe from ranging from four to sixty-four,4 - 64 Jess guides her clients to finding more ease and flow amongst the chaos of life.

Jess uses Instagram as her playground to share the magic of EFT.

Find Jess at www.instagram.com/thetappingspcae

Or check out her resources at www.thetappingspace.com.au

A LINE IN THE SAND

I had a plan. Get married, have babies, and get a job in Childcare. Simple, uneventful, peaceful. Perhaps hopeful, naïve, maybe even delusional.

I had all the typical signs of feeling pregnant and the three tests with two red lines on them. Yet, I still needed a doctor's assurance to validate it before allowing myself to truly believe it. When you have lost all belief in yourself, you feel you still need to get that backup from someone else. My self-esteem was so low, I 'didn't have faith in myself enough to believe the obvious.

I discovered I was having a girl, which filled me with wonder and childlike excitement. In the kaleidoscope of my life, the brightest and most amazing piece is the gift of my daughter choosing me to be her Mum. This was my line in the sand.

The day my beautiful baby girl was born, I'd like to say it was the happiest day of my life, but I found it quite traumatic. The nurses teased me with thoughts of some elusive positive pain, instead, it was excruciating levels of pure hell that went on seemingly forever. I recall the nurse coming in on Day One and looking lovingly at my newborn baby, "wasn't it all worth it?....I just cried.

I started to settle into my new role. Someone's Mother, protector, and lifeline. Undeniably, my daughter was perfect. I had so many dreams for us. It didn't occur to me not to dream. I named her Xanthe, and I couldn't wait to show her the world.

I could write a trilogy of my life, her life and our lives entwined. We have already spent a lifetime of so many emotions... wonderment, curiosity, excitement, sadness, relief, grief, hope, loneliness, absolute pride and pure joy.

In my mind, my plan was perfect. I would have a beautiful baby girl, explore the Universe together, and happily answer all of her questions. Children were always a part of my plans. They were a dream that I always felt would be a reality. The wonderment of being someone's Mum and all that it entailed.

I planned a childhood of adventures.... climbing trees, camping out under the stars, searching for smurfs under wild mushrooms, chasing fairies through dense forests. With every adventure came endless questions, and I'd answer each one of them. I'd point at the moon and make a wish upon falling stars. I'd explain the environment and share my joy of nature. It would all be so perfect.

In my heart, I knew that I would be a good Mum. But I wondered if I'd ever be ready. Would I ever feel "grown-up" enough? It was such a scary thought because I felt so young myself.

She was so pink when she was born, with plump little pink cheeks. Rated 9 on the Apgar scale, already a high achiever!

Over the months, the nurses were stunned by her development. She could walk assisted at three months and crawled at five months. As one nurse stated, "she's one to watch". As it turns out, she wasn't wrong in saying that. Unfortunately, I didn't really get a chance to brag about my little girl. Every new Mum feels pride and love; sharing milestones is part of the journey. My little butterfly was more advanced than all the other babies in my "new mummy support group", but I didn't like to talk about her milestones because I didn't want to look like I was "showing off".

One day though, she woke up, and something had changed within her. She wasn't standing in her cot saying "up" when I went in, and she wouldn't say "ta" for her toast. Something had changed, and I didn't know what or why. My baby girl was still very clever. She had an incredible talent for lining things up and clearly excellent organisational skills! She got lost in music, undoubtedly a budding Mozart! She would stare out the window and giggle, connecting at a higher level; so very spiritual! She loved watching the credits more than the show, maybe a scholar? I recall one of the other Mums laughing and commenting, "she's almost Autistic". Almost. That word doesn't soften the blow.

Deep down, I knew something was different. Why didn't my baby want to hug me? Or look at me? When the Paediatrician said, "we suspect that she has Autism", he was flippant. Like saying - the sky is blue, the grass is green, and I feel like a coffee. I stood there looking at him, waiting for information. Hope. Anything! But I got nothing. Except for a "come back in six months".

It was 2005, and thankfully, a lot has changed since then. I wasn't given any information about therapy, diet, or anything. So, it was up to me to research. Meanwhile, I was dealing with a disability (that I couldn't admit to myself) and newborn twins. I used to refer to it as "the A-word". I couldn't say Autism for a long time. Now I say it freely, live it, love it, own it!

I had depression and a debilitating anxiety disorder. It was a very challenging time. I wanted to hide from the world, home-school my children, and not go out. But with my little butterfly having "the A-word", I had to change my plans. I needed to be my daughter's voice and advocate for her. She pushed me out of my comfort zone, and as it turned out, I became worthy of that role.

I had thought about home-schooling my baby girl. However, it came from a place of fear and wanting to protect her, and it wasn't meant to be. The Universe can draw its line in the sand, a plot twist. Every butterfly needs to go through a process before it can spread its wings, and it turned out my little butterfly needed some extra help to spread hers. Finally, I couldn't hide any longer, and I had no choice but to come out of the darkness and be my daughter's light and voice. Little did I know that that was just the beginning of a lifetime of growing and learning.

My butterfly and I weren't given any hope. We were given labels but no hope or success stories to learn from. One professional even told me, "We can't do much with kids like this". And like all warrior mums, I didn't let that deter me! We created our own story of hope. My beautiful butterfly was considered non-verbal until she was eight years old, but now, in her words, she was "busy thinking". Isn't that so beautiful? Busy thinking.

Feeling trapped inside an unhappy marriage, I already felt isolated. But, when the Universe decided to challenge me with having a child with special needs, I reached a new level of isolation. My newborn twins were six weeks old when my daughter was diagnosed with a disability. Life was hectic. I lived under a veil that masked my sadness, silently pleading for help. I didn't know the rules. When was sad, sad enough? When was I allowed to leave? But if I did…. Where would I go? I had three babies in nappies, and one was a master escape artist. So, I stayed. It took another three years before I became a solo parent. Finally, I had no choice but to step up.

My baby boys surpassed their big sister in a few years, and Phoenix was always eager to please and would help me practice speech therapy with his sister on our travels to school. He was about three years old when I commented that he could be a Speech Therapist when he grows up, and in his cheery disposition, he replied, "No, Mummy, I want to be a Lollypop lady". Finally, after two years at the early intervention centre, it was time for my daughter to step into primary school. Mainstream schools couldn't accommodate her needs, so her journey into special school began. I wondered how I would explain to my boys that their sister was going to a new school, a school for children that have an intellectual disability. I was still coming to terms with it myself.

Walking into the school on that first day, my son asked, "Why is Xanthe going to "big school?" I could feel the lump form in my throat, and my mind raced, searching for the right words, when his little voice piped up again, "Is it because it's got a big roof?" "Yes, my darling…. because it's got a big roof!" It turns out that we don't always have to have the right answers. All that we need is acceptance and love. My beautiful children have been my greatest teachers of that lesson.

My little girl was non-verbal and had to use a seatbelt in class to help her stay seated. Her hand had to be always held when out; otherwise, she would run, and her safety would be at risk. She knew how to unlock a door and climb over a fence but hadn't yet learnt to stop at the edge of the road and check for cars.

The challenges were endless, but we faced each of them head-on! With no speech therapists in town, I held a big fundraising event to raise money to travel four hours on a train to have intensive therapy in the city. I tried everything…. diet, goji juice, vitamin supplements, programs that rewired the brain, anything and everything. The main thing was the determination of not giving up or settling. I wanted my daughter to have the best opportunity of living her best life, so with the support and encouragement of excellent teachers along the way, we kept raising the bar. Slowly but surely, my butterfly spread her wings, and she ended up graduating as School Captain.

I wanted more. I wanted to share my journey with others who understood a different kind of "normal". I wanted to be understood, and I needed support. Most of all, I wanted to give other people hope. I didn't want any other Mother to feel the same loneliness and despair that I felt. So, I created a group called Special Needs Fraser Coast, which has since been renamed *Disability Support Fraser Coast*. It's a support group for carers to discover, share and empower. If we can create a little light in other people's darkness, we're doing the right thing. So, my little group grew and is now an incorporated association run by a small but wonderful group of volunteers.

I've always loved having a volunteer role within the community, and it's one of my core values to help others less fortunate. I think we all have times in our lives when we could use a little help, and there are those times when we're able to help those around us. If we can shine our light to help guide the way for others on their journey, or if someone's light has dimmed, then it's a blessing to be able to remind them how amazing they are. I didn't do much, but I always got a lot out of what I did. Helping others helped me to feel less worthless.

In the darker times, I didn't think I would ever be anyone's true love. I didn't think I'd ever be able to work in a paid role. I recall a psychologist asking me once if I ever thought about re-joining the workforce, and the question spiralled me into an instant panic attack. Deep down, I always felt like a failure. I now know that that's something that depression tricks us into thinking. I was merely existing, waiting for my turn to die.

So much has changed since then. I was at the edge of a precipice and waiting for my time to end, but it didn't happen, so I thought, I might as well live. So, I drew a line in the sand, which was the start of a new beginning, a rebirth. I chose to heal. With help, I let go of the negative emotions attached to my past traumas but kept the learnings. My scared inner child was no longer haunting me. I felt as though I had finally stepped out of a fog, I didn't realise I was in. I felt alive, and it was incredible! When the world stopped in 2020, I used that time to study and became a practitioner so that I could help others heal. Once I had let go of the emotional baggage I'd been dragging along, and I had the chance to grow and spread my wings. It turned out that the world wasn't as scary as what I had created in my mind. After not working for nearly twenty years, I applied for two casual jobs. I didn't have a resume and my old boss from the last century (not even kidding, lol) was kind enough to be a referee. I stepped into the fear, and I succeeded. I landed both jobs, both in the Disability Industry. Again, my children have been my greatest teachers.

I went from victim to victory!! I stand here now, married to a fantastic man that treats me with the love and respect that I deserve. I'm employed and making a positive contribution to society. Being a Carer of a child with a disability or special needs can be very taxing, but it can bring you the most incredible abundance of joy that you could ever imagine. I've learnt to celebrate every single achievement in life, no matter how small. I embrace the joy and feel it with every inch of my being.

Now it's my turn to help others draw their line in the sand. Every single one of us deserves the chance to live our best life. We can't change the past, but we can change now. I can show others how to let go of trauma, create new goals and reach their dreams! I know what I am meant to do, and I know that my life would never have gone down this path if I hadn't been blessed with my precious daughter Xanthe. It's an enlightening lesson that I've only recently learnt: at any given moment, you can draw a line in the sand and create a new beginning. A *fresh new start* from here, right now, and it fills me with hope and a magical feeling of excitement.

In the past, it never even dawned on me that you could do that. My old script was filled with sadness, regret and loneliness. I would put my mask on so no one could see how I was feeling. Still, after years of doing that, it manifested into a deep depression and terrible, debilitating anxiety that left me suffocating. I was a victim. I held my secrets in the back of my mind, along with the accompanying shame, guilt, fear, sadness and anger. So many negative emotions are attached to stories of childhood abuse, domestic violence, and feelings of abandonment. I didn't realise that the person who had abandoned me was me.

Sometimes I allow myself to look back, but it's only to see how far I've come.

I am now the Queen of my castle and worthy of great love and respect. We all are.

So draw your line in sand and step into your fear, it's the short cut to creating **your** best life!

KAREN BAKER

Karen is passionate about helping and empowering others, especially carers. She loves people, knowing them, loving them, understanding them and helping them. Having a deep connection with another soul brings her spirit alive.

She has worked in several roles throughout the community within the Disability sector, including allied health, and peer facilitation. She held an Executive role on the special school P&C committee, organising many fundraising events. Karen is also the Founder and Director of *Disability Support Network Fraser Coast*, a not-for-profit organisation that supports families impacted by disabilities.

A long-time local of beautiful Hervey Bay in Queensland, she was blessed to marry her childhood crush and raise three amazing children. Karen likes to raise awareness to educate the broader community on disabilities and has been interviewed numerous times for articles on Autism for the local paper and magazines.

She has loved and lost, overcoming many obstacles of trauma and grief, but from that journey came love, empathy and understanding. She lives every day knowing that her Angels are there to guide her and reminds herself daily that we only have one chance at this life so be sure to leave a footprint.

Find Karen here - https://www.facebook.com/profile.php?id=100086594935902

WHAT TO EXPECT WHEN YOU GET WHAT YOU DIDN'T EXPECT

A s *A Course in Miracles* highlights, "everything we do is either love or a call for love," and the greatest miracle we can bless ourselves and those around us with, is a shift in our perception from fear to love, as only love exists.

My sincerest hope is that within this chapter, you will find comfort and guidance in knowing that everything is exactly as it is meant to be, and we truly have nothing to fear.

Dear God
Please show me, always, a way to return to my truth with grace and compassion, presence and commitment. When I've forgotten what I'm here to do, guide me home. Scaffold me in times of weakness and whisper to me softly to stay present.
I will never consciously stray from you.
Guide me home always, and I'll be forever grateful.

It started with a niggle, a middle-of-the-night awakening to what was landing in my consciousness, my thinking mind. Actually, let's scratch that; it started long before I even contemplated descending onto this earthly plane. In the last few years, my soul has rapidly evolved, my intuition strengthened, and my inner knowing combusted beyond my reasoning mind. Almost nine years ago, I birthed my first child; numb to my innate power, I willingly and knowingly handed over every decision about how I would bring her into the world. I remember driving to the hospital at thirty-eight weeks pregnant with a baby 'too big' for me to birth myself because 'I was too small' and saying to my husband, "I don't even know why we are doing this, she is not ready, and when the time is right, I will do it. But I guess we better do it because if something happens, it will be, I told you so". Transitioning from maiden to mother was hard; nonetheless, it was necessary for my growth and to become who I am today. All of our experiences are. They awaken us to the truth of who we are, God-consciousness. Divine light. Unlimited and pure.

For my second child, I empowered myself. I enlisted in all the external support I needed and practised hypnobirthing for months leading up to her birth. We decided to call her Kahli, after the Goddess Kali. We decided this before she was born, or more so, her chosen name came to us. For her birth, I was empowered, active, happy and capable. Her bouncy ten-pound four-ounce voluptuous body easily and intuitively entered the birth portal when the time was right, and we, her humble parents, welcomed her to earth. Little did I know at the time that Kali, The Goddess of fire and destruction, the name we had blissfully and subconsciously given our chubby babe, would unravel my ego at the speed of light.

Everything changed. I would often sit and look at my calm, sweet, hungry-for-knowledge firstborn and my fierce, feisty, tender-loving second born and think I was different. I could not go back to who I was. I had evolved. However, birthing a baby with a disability has been my greatest evolution to date. Life feels the same, but nothing will ever be the same again.

After years of making decisions based on an inner knowing or feeling, without evidence or often common sense ("I just feel it, I just know it, I can see it"), I reached a point where I woke in the middle of the night with a niggle to have a third baby. The presence of this powerful soul was with me with every waking and sleeping minute for what felt like an eternity. Trust has been a big thing; it's easy to believe that God is great and has a plan but trusting and surrendering into that is another thing! I was exhausted from the niggle, the persistence of it, the excitement of the prospect and the fear of which decision to make. So, with that at the forefront, I took a mental health day and decided to climb a mountain about two hours away, again because of inner direction and guidance, to clear my mind and ground myself in mother nature. I dropped the girls off at day care and headed off. The climb was beautiful, and I felt very adventurous and brave.

That day though, something drastic happened. I was entering the descent, and I slipped. On the way down, the coils of a tree stump wrapped around a big boulder snapped, and I started to slide. I was hanging on for dear life, literally, at the side of this mountain. I phoned my husband, who could barely hear me with the wind, to say goodbye (he was none the wiser that I was not at work and indeed thought it was a prank), and I stood there and listened. I took a deep breath and closed my eyes. Then the wind stopped. I climbed back up and tucked myself under an overhanging rock. I looked at this perfectly round boulder, without an ounce of leverage to take me up and thought, "well fuck, thanks God. Now do I not only die, but you would rather me perish instead of fall and die". I still cannot, to this day, recall how I scaled the boulder to get up and out. I do know, however, that I got to the top and vomited. With divine timing, the mountain rangers came down and were surprised to see me. Not half as surprised as I was to see the clear, smack-in-your-face signs of which way to go on your descent. I pretended I was all good, casually chilling out, before following them down. When I got to my car, I was still shaking, I turned off my radio to sit and be still, and it mysteriously turned back on, playing, *'The time is now.'*

So, I listened. I heard and felt what was coming through and knew I needed to have a serious conversation with my husband.

I answered the niggle (or we did!), the call, and the persistence. But, oh, my darling baby, I knew. I knew she was coming with big lessons. The lessons that we needed to learn in this lifetime. The ones that are and will continue to awaken our souls and bring forth evolution

67

beyond our wildest dreams. The lessons that would empower us to look at the shadows or remain resistant in the murky waters of worry and anxiety. At the very core of my essence, I knew she was coming to shake us up and teach us. And I knew my other two darling daughters were prepping and priming me.

Nine months later, sweet baby Bonnie, all ten-pound-four ounces of her, was welcomed into the loving embrace of her family at home in the birth pool, wedged into our tiny fixer-upper. She was so perfect, with soft velvety skin and a smooshy face. Within a week, we travelled over 1000 km for breastfeeding support and returned home hoping to settle into our fourth trimester. However, things were about to unravel for us. A slight eye twitch that I had noticed on day three bugged me. Intuitively I knew it wasn't innocent. I mentioned it to my husband and sister, but neither of them witnessed it. A couple of days later, I noticed body shivers, as if Bonnie was cold or having repetitive startle reflexes and beckoned my sister to record them. My sister tried to reassure me to stay focused on getting Bonnie feeding well and go from there. Our local hospital, not equipped for neurological presentations, arranged for us to be airlifted to Queensland Children's Hospital (QCH). It will be forever etched in my mind, seeing my baby bundled into an incubator for the trip. There was so much of everything, people, things, noise, beeping, syringes and tears. After numerous tests, EEGs, an MRI and blood tests, we were released on Christmas Eve, believing this may be something Bonnie may grow out of. "Hallelujah, our prayers have been answered!" I thought.

Sadly, we were transported by ambulance back to the hospital on Christmas morning and transferred again to QCH. This time, the doctors did some genetic testing and administered medications. Over the coming weeks, Bonnie's myoclonic seizures progressed into Infantile Spasms (also known as West Syndrome), which involve a hypsarrhythmia, whereby her entire brain was in chaos twenty-four-seven, which was causing her to have crunch-like spasms with gut-wrenching baby whimpers in between. At this point, the action was fast and hard. Not only was Bonnie's brain in chaos, but her development was on hold or deteriorating rapidly. Bonnie had not opened her eyes in weeks. I remained stuck, wanting to trade my life for hers but riddled with guilt for my other two phenomenal children, my moon and stars. I cried and cried in my mother's arms, selfishly wondering what the best outcome in this situation would be for us all. So on my knees, I stayed and prayed. "For the love of God, let me see this situation differently".

Storm: verb: to move forcefully in a specified direction.

As I lay in the bedside chair with my sweet naked babe at my breast, listening to the torrential storm roll over our heads, I knew this time was different. I had accidentally given my darling girl five millilitres of a super hard drug instead of 0.5ml the night before, which saw my husband and I do a midnight dash to the hospital. As I walked across the garden to wake the grandparents and gently roused the girls to relocate into our family bed, I knew this time was different. Tonight was either going to go one of two ways. How could I have mistaken the amount, even if the label was dodgy? I had not missed a beat with an intensive medication administration regime in eleven weeks. How could I have made this mistake? I don't believe in coincidences. I believe in a faithful unfolding of life events and divine guidance.

I told my husband, "I have heard twelve weeks repetitively for weeks now," throughout this journey. What will happen at twelve weeks? I thought. I had many reassuring signs that "a turning point, the road to recovery will begin". Will she be ok? I asked, "Yes, but it'll be a bumpy road nonetheless, so suck the marrow and find the joy."

It was as if the storm passing overhead, on the cusp of a new moon and the precipice of the twelve-week mark of Bonnie Mae, there was clearing in our path. We were mid-air, Bonnie swollen and bloated from the steroids, puffy and pale. The weather became eerily dark and miserable, and then the sun was blinding through the clouds. It was extraordinary. The skies cleared, and it felt like a washing away of debris and cleansing our hearts of unwanted burdens. I felt calm. She felt calm- the epitome of calm. This time I knew I was travelling with more hope and less fear, more love and less rage, more guidance and less pessimistic chitter chatter. I was travelling with my sunshine.

On the twelve week mark, after three months of seizures, infantile spasms, EEGs, heart rate monitors, spinal taps, hourly or bi-hourly medication administration, relentless vomiting from said seizures and spasms, hospital admissions, blood pressure and urine samples multiple times a week, insatiable appetite due to significantly high steroid treatment, immunity compromisation, mastitis, tongue tie releases, arching, cannula after cannula, up and down, highs and lows, counting and counting, and a rushed baptism because we feared the worse, and all while my baby barely opened her eyes, we were given our diagnosis. Bonnie hasSTXBP1. This condition is rare and complex, with a genetic mutation occurring on the 9th chromosome resulting in epilepsy and development complications. The spectrum is vast and sweeps across motor, speech and overall development. Currently, no cure is available, and there is no identified treatment.

I don't think I will ever forget the faces of my family, my husband and my children, as we received this news. The sound of their hearts breaking into a thousand pieces, thinking, "this is not what we expected nor wanted; this is not how it is supposed to be". I wanted a pram park, not a disability one. I had plans for my maternity leave, including beachside hangs, not hospital bed hanging on. They wanted a sister, a baby they could cuddle and hide in the warmth of their blankets, not take turns in seizure-watching. I questioned God, "why are we being punished? We are good people, aren't we?".

Quite rapidly, the vision was clear; this is precisely what we signed up for, albeit without awareness. This is our energetic contract, our sacred blueprint. I remember my eldest daughter comforting me in our dilapidated kitchen one day and uttering the words, "mum this will be ok; God is looking out for us. Bonnie is a child of God's. This is not happening to us, but for us. We can do this". And she was right. My wise little nine-year-old was shining back to me, the light I have always carried.

I knew long before we conceived Bonnie that life would change; we would be complete, whole, and at peace. Did I know it would look like this? Absolutely not. But I knew God was instrumental in every action I have taken, every experience I have encountered, the training I have undertaken, connections I have made, and support I have placed in my life until this moment. I know that deep within, I would never have chosen this life - the path of disability, a medically complex diagnosis, and uncertainty. I would never have consciously chosen whether to do intensive training for my special needs child during school holidays or spend two weeks with my neuro typically developing children. I would never have chosen it for my daughter Bonnie, my husband David or our other two children.

But the sense of freedom within my soul is vast. The freedom in not following the 'norm', living beyond the labels and limitations, and finding joy in "not fitting in". The opportunity to lay down the ego and the "what will people think" and to see only love. The smiles, the middle of the night bab babs, the kicking, the extra cautious caretaking of two older protective sisters and the sheer delight that my workaholic husband relishes in the slower than the speed of lighting growth patterns of our other two children. A dear friend and mentor said to me, during my darkest days of trying to grasp onto what was happening, "Bonnie chose this, she is the one who sacrificed showing up in this body to teach you". And whilst this may be contrary to popular belief, it marries well with "our children are our greatest teacher", a mantra I have spouted long before I became a mother myself.

"When the student is ready, the teacher will appear", Buddha.

If you have been entrusted as the caretaker of an extraordinary child, a medically complex future filled with worries and doubts, please know this - you are safe, everything will be ok, all we see is the past, so in this present moment, be open to the miracle. Know that love and light are on the other side of your fear, stress, worry, and anxiety (which is valid and worthy of recognition). Find joy and happiness and freedom to be in the present moment and live in the now. Recognise that as painful as this may be right now, and trust me, I get it; there is always hope—life within life, life after life. Our physical presentations are the

71

least interesting aspect about our children and us. This is your Sacred Blueprint. This is the work you and I are here to do. There is an opportunity amidst the despair to dismantle the term disability; I mean, who is more disabled, my child who smiles nonstop in a perceived "disabled body", or me, in a perceived healthy body, often crippled by my ego, worries, anxiety or sweating the small stuff.

So, what do we do when we get what we are not expecting? We surrender our ego. There is simply nothing we can control. Turn inwards to your heart space and find love. Allow love to consume you at every opportunity. And project that out to every other soul you encounter on this uncertain path.

I share this prayer with you, one I found deep comfort in at the time when I was on my knees questioning everything.

"Lord, grant me the grace of Wonder. Rather than fearing change and the unknown, let me embrace the unknown with a sense of Wonder. Instead of closing down and fearing the worst, let the grace of Wonder open my imagination and my senses. Life runs in cycles. All things come to an end, yet every end means a new beginning. Beginnings are filled with opportunities to make different choices, to reboot, and start anew. Lord, let the grace of Wonder flow abundantly in my psyche and soul, especially during the time when I feel most vulnerable" ~ Intimate Conversations with the Divine by Caroline Myss

LARA WILLIAMS

Lara is a mother, advanced intuitive guide and founder of sacred blueprint. She is here to help those with extraordinary needs and abilities discover their life purpose and bridge the gap between their physical and metaphysical worlds, so they can shine their joy and limitless love on the world.

As a self-proclaimed student of life, she has spent her years devoted to learning from and serving some of the most vulnerable souls within our community, our children. Lara worked in child protection for over a decade before embarking on her journey to become a trauma informed embodiment coach. She uses her god conscious awareness, innate intuition, her training and experience to journey beyond the physical realm and unveil the sacred blueprint between parent and child.

Since becoming a mother to three spirited girls, her own journey of discovery has accelerated. Especially since her youngest daughter, Bonnie was born with a rare genetic mutation, igniting Lara with even more passion to live a full, abundant and sacred life.

Lara lives in Hervey Bay, Queensland with her husband David and their three girls. Whilst Lara is adept in her field at connecting parents and children together on the deepest level, she also is magnetic and humorous in her delivery. She is known to seek joy in every moment, finding magic in the *Mum-dane,* all the while knowing her service is her medicine.

Find and connect with Lara here:
https://www.facebook.com/attunedcaring
www.instagram.com/attunedcaring

JOEL'S #SHITUATION

"*There is no education like adversity*"- *Benjamin Disaraeli*
I have always wanted to write a book about parts of my life, and I even had a title of what I thought captured my life perfectly, 'You 'can't make this shit up!' Often when discussing snippets of my life to people (yes, I am an oversharer), they would have this look of disbelief on their faces, where I would assure them, I was telling the truth as you literally can't make this shit up. Sadly, for me, Kevin Hart stole my title minus the swear word and wrote a hilarious book, so I can't even be that mad. The next best thing to writing a whole book is the invitation to contribute to this extraordinary book that I know will be an emotional roller coaster for readers and contributing authors alike. My next problem is where to start.

There are many components to this story, but all revolve around one young man, born eighteen years ago in 2004, who was diagnosed at roughly fifteen months with Angelman Syndrome. This young man was one of the most wanted, prayed-for babies ever born. I know every parent thinks that, but after losing four babies, two girls and two boys, to a condition known as Potters Sequence, he was the miracle baby we thought would make our life complete. So, lets go a bit further back.

I was born in Malaysia as my Dad was in the RAAF, and I grew up in sunny Queensland. My early memories of life were good. I had an annoying little brother one year younger, and growing up, we were free-range kids exploring our neighbourhood and nearby creeks with friends all day. I grew into an awkward teen who was very lost and started to rebel (against what I still do not know to this day). Then at sixteen, I was offered an opportunity to take on a governess position in Kalgoorlie, in Western Australia, looking after four of my gorgeous young cousins at a large station an hour out of town. This was where I met the father of all my children at the age of seventeen.

I had my eldest daughter Kaitlin at the age of nineteen while living on a different station, and approximately a year later, we moved to Perth, where not long after, I found out I was pregnant again, which was a shock as I was breastfeeding and on the mini pill. The pregnancy caused a rift in the relationship, and I moved back to Queensland with my young baby for family support. At a twenty-week ultrasound, I found out my baby did not have kidneys and would not survive. I felt alone and bereft in my grief. By that time, the father had come to terms with the pregnancy and wanted to resume the relationship but was still in WA. I was told I had to be induced, and in shock and grief with my mother by my side, I delivered a stillborn little girl named Kasey. I was young and emotional and had no idea what I was doing or what to expect. That experience has forever haunted me, and I wish I had known a lot more and done things differently. The health system does not cater well for situations like this. Instead, I was told, 'it was just one of those tragic things that happened' and 'not likely ever to happen again' . How very wrong that was.

I moved back to WA not long after. Fast forward eight years. There were babies everywhere, and one of my dearest friends had just had a gorgeous little girl. My heart ached every time I held her, I felt empty and hollow, and the longing grew. Having my eldest helped with the grief, but I desperately wanted another baby. We decided we would like to try again. Time had helped with the grief, and I wanted to give my daughter the sibling she had been asking for. Falling pregnant came easily for me. At an antenatal appointment, we were told that

Potters Sequence could be genetic. We had only found out a couple of years before that the children's father only had one kidney. At the nineteen-week scan, it was revealed this little girl also had no kidneys. I was devastated, shocked, incredulous and again induced. The process repeated of giving birth to my second stillborn baby girl, who we named Chiara. We sought genetic counselling and were given a 50/50 chance of this happening again. Honestly, I became obsessed with wanting another baby and could not get the thought out of my head. It was irrational, and I thought surely this could not happen again after two losses. Two baby boys, Blake and Jake, were born without breath, and my head space was not great.

I was angry at the world and was jealous of every person I saw holding a baby. I bargained, prayed, drank too much alcohol and had very bitter thoughts. Finally, we decided to try one more time, and that was it. I would move on and accept the outcome, whatever the universe had decided. I grew up Catholic and no longer believed in a God, especially one who could do this to my family. Then finally, at the twenty-week ultrasound, the doctor gave me the news I had prayed to the universe for. My baby had two working kidneys. I sobbed. I never cried at the previous ultrasounds, I shed my tears in private. This time I cried tears of pure joy. My happiness could not be shattered.

I was truly ecstatic. Joel was induced four days early and born on the 22 of July 2004. This baby boy did not sleep well, had reflux that saw me covered in vomit for the first year of his life and struggled with feeding, but I was very happy. He was such a smiley baby, and everyone remarked how happy he was. The only concern was that he was not quite meeting his milestones. It was becoming more evident with time. You are told not to compare your child to others, but each week at the local playgroup, it was becoming harder not to notice the widening gap. During a visit to Queensland, my mother voiced her concerns after we visited a cousin with a baby of a similar age, and I knew it was not something we could ignore any longer.

We were referred to a Paediatrician, and the testing began. For some reason, I will never know, we were sent to a neurologist. By this stage, I was pregnant again. Yes, an oopsy baby, and we had also just had the exciting news that she had two kidneys. This time of my life is all a bit of a blur, but we went to the neurologist with our beautiful happy baby boy, and he asked me if Joel was always this happy. I beamed with pride and told him yes; he hardly ever cried and was always smiling and happy. He said the words that shook my world and changed my life in so many ways 'I think your son has Angelman Syndrome'. I came home numb, in shock and heartbroken. I googled Angelman Syndrome. My heart sank knowing the neurologist was correct, and the tears flowed for hours. My son's father told me that he did not think it was Angelman Syndrome as he was missing several of the features listed and had never had a seizure. I knew the neurologist was right in my heart, and one of the main features, a happy demeanour, was the dead giveaway. The blood tests came back, and it was indeed Angelman Syndrome. Joel has a deletion in the gene known as UBE3A on his 15th chromosome.

I thought I was bitter and angry before Joel's diagnosis, but I was now feeling red hot, explosive rage. How could this happen, had we not suffered enough? What had I done to deserve this? Why the hell me? It was so damn shitty and unfair. I was critical and judging of anyone I felt undeserving of children. Then if one more person said, 'God only gives special children to special people' and other unhelpful cliches, I was likely to thump them no matter how well-intentioned! I held on to that anger for a very long time, and it still does surface now and then; we are human. I know now that this emotion has never really served any useful purpose. Through a lot of self-discovery, reading and reflection, I have found far more useful emotional tools that do help.

I learnt that Angelman Syndrome is a condition that occurs in approximately 1:15000, although with better testing, it may be a higher number. Deletion is not the only mechanism; other types causing Angelman Syndrome are Mutation, Imprinting Centre Defect, Uniparental Disomy, and Mosaic. Some children receive a clinical diagnosis if they have all the characteristics without the genetic component. Angleman Syndrome characteristics include global developmental delay, impaired movement and balance, lack of speech, seizures, feeding and sleep difficulties. Two of the features that stand out are their happiness and love of water. Parents and families with Angelman Syndrome can spot another Angelman child often based on these two characteristics alone. There are varying levels of impairment, and each child is very individual in how they present. Some can run and jump. Others have words or signs. Some AS children are unable to walk and require a lot of care. As with everything, there is no one size fits all and people living with Angelman Syndrome have abilities as comprehensive as they are varied. For a better understanding, there are a few videos on the website https://angelmansyndrome.org/angelman-syndrome . Proud Mama moment: Joel is in a few of them and is a cutie.

Occasionally I will refer to people with Angelman Syndrome as Angels because, like most Aussies, we tend to shorten everything. Not because our children are Angels, as they often have a little devil inside them. Children with Angelman Syndrome can appear angelic, like all children at times but also seem to have a cheeky, more mischievous side and are known to have poo parties & create #shituations beyond description. You cannot turn your back for one minute as they wait patiently, 'angelically' for that very moment and create havoc despite many having limited mobility! When Joel was younger and unable to walk, he could still roll, crawl or climb at astonishing speed, could find a puddle through the dog door, or turn on a tap while sitting in a sink with complete ease. He certainly kept us on our toes.

While having a diagnosis was a relief, it helped me understand which therapies may benefit Joel and where to focus. At this point, I was exhausting myself through various therapies that I now know were not beneficial. That wonderful old chestnut of hindsight and everybody doing the best they could with what they knew at the time, which was not a lot! We could now target those therapies that would help Joel build strength and improve his quality of life. I longed to meet other families with the syndrome and reached out to a beautiful mother named Liz, who had an older daughter with Angelman Syndrome. She drove over to meet me, and I asked so many questions. She was kind and patient and told me to slow down. This was one of the first of many amazing friendships I have made on the special needs journey.

The physiotherapist mentioned one day that she knew of another younger family with a little boy of a similar age on the north side, and we arranged a meeting. Little did I know that there would be three young 'Angels' there; two boys and one girl, all born within a year of each other. Joel was the youngest. I literally found my tribe that day. It was pure relief to have this 'Angel' family who completely got it. We all shared similar fears, frustration, triumphs, sadness and hope. The laughter was the best medicine, and we laughed a lot. Our four ended up in the same class for a few years doing conductive education, which was brilliant for our children's learning and 'interesting' for their lovely teachers. Our tribe grew, and we met more families who helped us navigate this unknown journey. We formed the WA Angelman Syndrome Association and continued to advocate for our children and a more promising future. I met many more amazing families through Joel's school and made many special friendships. Unfortunately, we also experienced loss, and I have attended many children's funerals. This is one of the hardest things about belonging to the special needs community.

Joel developed seizures three weeks before his third birthday. He just started taking up to three steps and then had severe swelling in his knees. He was diagnosed with Juvenile Idiopathic Arthritis (JIA), another cruel blow that stopped him from walking until 2013. Over the next few years, he was in and out of the hospital frequently for various issues and broke bones easily. My marriage was broken, and the father had removed himself entirely from our lives. My youngest daughter Amiel developed post-strep nephritis and was so excited at the age of five to be in the hospital as it was her turn, not her brother's. This was a meaningful reminder of how disability impacts siblings, and I realised how many buckets I was trying to fill at once. She took blood pressure medication for a year and loved her hospital stay. After further hospitalisations I felt I could no longer remain in WA with such a limited support network. My workplace was wonderful, but it all became too much on my own, and my family encouraged my move back to Queensland.

I came home and shared a place with my amazingly supportive, no longer quite so annoying brother, Carl. He did not do 'poonami's' or 'poonado's but was fantastic in every other way. In fact, during a #shituation the whole place cleared out! My parents, thankfully, were down the road and with their support and help, I enrolled in a nursing degree. I wanted to give back. I don't know how I did it, and many assignments were done bedside in the emergency department. I met some great people at university that encouraged me. There were many times I wanted to throw it all in. I also met my now husband Kieran in 2012, who became one of my most incredible supporters. He also has two beautiful daughters. I got my dream job in a busy paediatric tertiary hospital in the emergency department, where I continue to learn something new every shift. I am also eternally grateful for the perspective it has given me. As hard as I think my life is, some are doing it tougher. Sometimes, small things like the offering of a cup of tea can make the difference for those families. Life continues to be crazy and hectic. Our blended family has been through a lot, and females outweigh my husband, including two cats and two dogs.

There are many promising therapies being developed that could potentially change 'Joel's life and many others with rare diseases. It feels like it is no longer a dream to hope that one day Joel will have a better quality of life, but almost a certainty, which fills my heart with so much joy. The unrelenting work and determination of parents and families working together to raise awareness, and money for research, has shown that it takes just one person to create a ripple effect that has the power to make a momentous difference for the lives of many.

Joel is now eighteen and non-verbal. He can be stubborn and determined and often requires two people to help with his cares. Joel will always require around-the-clock care. If I could change one aspect of his life it would be communication. We know a lot of what he wants, but I want to hear him speak. To say 'I love you'. I know he does as he wraps me in bear hugs and plonks all seventy kilos on my lap, and follows me around like a puppy. I want him to be able to tell me he has an annoying wedgie or is sick of pasta salad. I want to know where he hurts, if his stomach is sore or has a headache. It is so difficult and frustrating trying to guess what is going on both physically and emotionally. Imagine that you were trapped in your body and never able to tell somebody what you wanted, needed?

I still do not know if I have found my exact purpose in life as I feel there is something very important I am meant to be doing, but I feel trapped by the limiting beliefs I am holding on to. However, I have managed to run a half marathon in a tutu, attend a gala dinner in Chicago, and raise funds in numerous ways for Angelman Syndrome. I have served on the committee for several years, and helped organise conferences over the years. My big dream, however, is to create a respite house for parents like myself who are caught between 'no man's land' and don't fit any of the 'normal' conventional respites. Somewhere where families could come and stay separately if they wished, and be close by while relaxing, and refilling their very depleted self-care buckets. I know as hard as life has been, we have had so many wonderful opportunities because of this extraordinary young man, and I am grateful for all the friendships, travel and learning opportunities I have been given. Watch this space.

LYSANDRA CALLAHAN

Lysandra is a disability advocate, and nurse in a major paediatric tertiary hospital. Her passion and purpose for supporting children and families was catalysed by her extraordinary life.

Mother to three living children, two stepdaughters and two grand-daughters, Lysandra's start in motherhood was anything but ordinary. She has lost four babies to a rare genetic disorder called Potters Sequence, and then her son Joel (the inspiration for this chapter) was born. Joel was diagnosed at fifteen months old with Angelman Syndrome.

Joel is the reason for Lysandra's career change to nursing, and why she advocates for disability. She is a committee member for the Angelman Syndrome Association of Australia and is on the frontline with helping newly diagnosed families in Queensland to navigate their journey.

Lysandra lives with her wonderfully supportive, outnumbered husband Kieran, on the outskirts of Brisbane with their menagerie of animals including dogs, cats, fish and 18 chickens. In her rare spare time, she loves to hike, travel and read.

Find Lysandra at www.instagram.com/lysandraw1
www.linkedin.com/in/lysandra-callahan-05220ab0

MY ONLY ENEMY IS ME

"It was when I died, I felt the most alive. At the death of all my attachments and limitations, I stumbled across utter peace. A moment etched in time; it was only when I stopped strangling and let go of my life that I found the essence of being alive, to be."
Mason Damian

Let me start by asking you this question. Is there something in your life that is deep, that calls for attention, or your awareness? It may be hidden within the cracks or right in your face. Is there an event, experience, habit or emotion that scrambles your identity, your purpose? It often feels like this intense part of ourselves has knocked us off our path to a goal or any chance of happiness. Yet, if the path was the only way to move forward, and if something is placed on our path, it is not blocking it; it becomes the path. It is there to strengthen your existence going forward, not belittle it or make it stuck. I wanted so badly to look away and forget about it, but the lessons were there to enhance my experience and give me new wisdom on how to approach every aspect and moment of my life differently. The Universe, everything, is a teacher and works in the most mysterious ways. When we shift our perspective, a lesson becomes a gift. The funny thing about a lesson is that you only understand it afterwards. That is the beautiful point when we see what our chaos was once, is actually the steppingstone to personal liberation. For me, this was an existential endeavour into the meaning or mystery that is life, human life in this case. A riddle that would tear me into two but bring me back together in the form of a new self.

The strangest part of my journey was remembering that I was a happy child, free in imagination, unbeknownst to darkness and limitations. My beliefs and sense of self were free flowing without rigidness. My sense of identity and attachment to the world was something to share at this point, not mine. I could pretend to be anyone or anything and then nothing at the same time. That's why we can role play so easily as a child because we know it's a role and that it's play but taking on a serious persona (an act) is so confusing for a child. I had a great child-hood and now see that life was this way as a child because I was not exposed to the darkness, and I couldn't bind the opposites with meaning once I was.

As I rummaged through the purposeless school system and saw all my friends' psychological shift, I held my feelings inside. I saw the change inside me and others to take life seriously and to fit into the machine that was knocking at my door. I began analysing the world pretty early on, and I never stopped questioning everything about human life. I felt like no one knew what we were doing, and we didn't even know why we were doing it. I didn't open up because either everyone felt the same and never said anything, or I was the only one feeling it.... I didn't know which was scarier, so I thought I couldn't share the dark nature of my condition. I cared for the collective as an extension of myself. After poor attempts to gain love or excitement in what I was told would bring me love and excitement, I seemed to fall short every time. At this point, I knew where I was heading; I felt the world had already pushed it onto me, suicide. Until this point, life was like I was on a very slow conveyor belt towards death, because each day I felt the same things from the days before. I tried to fill my hole with the same things everyone else was, material pleasures. My lack of self-love and purpose led me to seek out impermanent joy and happiness, from drugs to sex, entertainment even, and gaming. I was a black hole. I could have latched onto anything in this era for an escape, yet I ended up back where I was.

I knew I was doing the right thing because I followed my heart. I felt real things, real emotions in the darkness because that was my vision. I always saw a different civilisation possible, one at the forefront of knowledge, freedom and peace for all. The material game was a shambles if we did not even know our existence or have a goal to move towards. I couldn't throw myself into the unknown without purpose. All these thoughts alienated me on Earth, so I eventually planned to take my life. I was at a point where I didn't want to continue. I was eighteen years old, and I saw no point in going on to do anything if I felt this way. I found a drug dealer who sold Xanax, and I ordered a large amount and decided to consume it with alcohol, a known deadly concoction. The feelings I experienced leading up to this event were so freeing; there was a dark pleasure in doing something so treacherous. Now I was a ghost walking around, I was no one, and I had no worries. It was a sick joke that I experienced happiness when I was going to die, yet that did not stop me.

It was the 6th of September 2019, I had the deal planned to pick it up finally, and I was so nervous but still so sure. I walked out of my house, and to my surprise, my father had just gotten home. I was looking down in a rush to my car, and he hopped out of the car, and I told him I was just going down the road. My stomach sank, and even now, it is a moment that is deep in the heart of both of us. I knew what I was doing to him, and I still had to do it anyway. I left and picked up what I ordered; I turned my phone on silent to make it easier. To deny my existence as if I was already gone. I drove out to a spot where my friends and I would go to smoke. As I parked my car in some native bushlands, I began consuming up to twenty-five pills of Xanax along with alcohol, cannabis and nitrous oxide. I was listening to my favourite songs until it eventually felt like I entered a coma; I cannot remember going unconscious. From this point, I have only snapshots of images. The next day my friends and family were trying to find me;

miraculously enough, I parked in a spot where they were doing back burning, and the police were notified. I remember being helped into my car and the officer searching the car and asking me questions. I was shocked that I now had to face what I had done. From glimpses of the back of the police car to home and then the hospital, I don't remember much of that day but waking up in the hospital. I was handed papers suggesting or "diagnosing" that I had Borderline Personality Disorder (BPD), which seemed like a viable answer to my family, but I knew it was all me. Then next, they put me into a mental ward, and I begged my parents to let me out before leaving that first night.

Being in the ward reinforced the fact that I was stuck with this mind-less society that I had outgrown and that if I was going to find peace, it was up to me. I was so angry that I was alone in my awareness, and no one could cure it. There were many ups and downs, but somehow, I continued to drag myself through after attempting suicide. I still resented the world and took it all as a serious attack, but now I couldn't blame the world any longer. Instead, I began to blame myself for what I had just put myself through. I began to see what I was doing to myself despite the world going on in the background. But I couldn't let go, and now I had to feel this way when I didn't even want to be here in the first place. I tried my best with what I had at the time. I cherished my rich friendships and relationships that held space for me, my dark thoughts, and those who understood me. But this was still my journey to conquer alone.

I did not see how I could shift my perspective so much that I could move forward with a new mindset, but I knew it was the only answer. Unfortunately, I had not explored my options at this point, so I was doomed to repeat my pain on myself time and time again until I finally ran myself down. Then, finally, when I was so jaded from my endless mental torture, at the perfect synchronisation, I could take the path to peace when it arose. I jumped at it the same way I did my suicide because, honestly, I was not seeking more pain; I was seeking peace. And you cannot create something new with the same mindset you created the old. You cannot add more pain to find peace; a part of me knew that. If the attempt and the ward taught me anything, it showed me that I could change.

It was now May 2020, and I still sought death as my only solution, yet when I had LSD this one night, it showed me how quickly reality could change. I stayed up all night trying to understand reality if it was not fixed. The experience left me with a thirst to do it again to understand how I could detach and enjoy myself. So, I took it again, not even two days later. This time after the shift in my perception, I was eager to investigate the experience again. I wanted to learn what exactly I was and how I was influenced by the world, my emotions and my thoughts. This time, like the first, I felt the presence of a higher being within me, like the spirit of Mother Earth was slithering through my skin. It was a ceremony like what the shamans would do in their tribes worldwide with psychedelics. I was shedding back layers, being tested on this night to see how strong my awareness was. If I could overcome fears in the mind on LSD, I could do it normally with my own life. After going back and forth with this new perspective, I was called to put on a guided meditation after having such a spiritual experience on this psychedelic.

I read the name Alan Watts, and somehow it already felt familiar. So, I listened to it. This man spoke of the mysteries of life with such plea-sure, and he showed me how to experience myself without judgment and limitations. He spoke in ways I would talk to myself in my head about myself, which freaked me out. He spoke wisdom that would change my life in an instant. Before, I focused on my whole life and everything I was attached to, and he showed me the present moment. A place without identity. It was during the meditation I experienced it but only guided. Afterwards, I would sit up after lying down for the meditation and immediately go back to my depressed state. This man just shook my world and showed me a path, and I went straight back. But now, what he showed me was in my awareness, so when I approached these thoughts, I did it on the last whim of my old aware-ness. I knew that focusing on the past would not improve things. I then learnt to see that my focus was what was bringing me pain because when Alan had just brought me into the present, I didn't experience it.

The room fell quiet, my girlfriend on the bed sleeping, my anxiety ever present. I then looked at myself and asked, why do I not feel okay right now? Mason, no one is looking at you, no one is pressuring you, and nothing in the world is influencing your state of being right now but you. And then it clicked. It all did at once; I had been fooling myself. I gave myself the poison I was sick of drinking.

No matter what has happened, you must find a way to engage with the present moment because the present moment is without the illusion of what is not in your experience at the current time. At that moment, I saw that I could give myself peace, not just in that moment of detachment but in every moment of my life. I learnt that every moment is a fresh beginning. We can redefine ourselves anew each moment. I did not now see a vengeful past but a loving one. One that had brought me to this very moment. I laughed tremendously when I found the present moment, where I would finally live without illusion.

As you can imagine, my guilt and shame diminished, and I began to look at everything differently, learning the faculties of my own consciousness. I was now a pure observer. I could play any role seriously if I tried or any thought or emotion. My essence was my awareness; if I became aware of that, I would now be more careful about what I focus on and why. What I bring into that awareness is what I become. Life was now becoming a spiritual experience, and it was my own creation. It was not just something happening to me. I felt complete unity, a part of the process of the Universe, not a visitor. The feeling of nirvana this night eventually led me down the spiritual path after my pain began healing and my wisdom began to expand.

I could now learn from life with focus and intent, and I began to see synchronicity after having a meaningless experience. I could now embrace the present moment and live life without resisting it. I could now watch it beautifully unfold with faith and self-control.

"We must abandon completely the notion of blaming the past for any kind of situation we're in."
Alan Watts

The Law of Impermanence states that nothing is permanent, and the self is not excluded from that law. As our environment changes, we must learn to adapt. As you grow, you realise that your ability to control yourself within uncontrolled situations is your power; it's you. You cannot find everlasting happiness; you must create it. Instead of seeing it through black and white, through the lens of social engineers, we can learn to approach things in our own way. Be serious here; softer over here. Instead of reacting, we use awareness to recognise our emotions without becoming them. From this place, we can respond in each moment; with a breath of relaxation and discernment, and our emotions become information we can sift through instead of immediately becoming them. And by doing this, we are creating a new reality where there are no words or limitations to anything that's happening. After all, this is your world, so it makes sense for you to create it yourself; then, you will have your own meaning. Because that's where the real stuff is, where your life begins, where it thrives. Thinking is good but only in balance with not thinking and stillness, like how an action is useless without rest. It is unnatural to think all the time. Not anticipating is a healthy form of therapy, releasing our grip on the world. Thinking is useless if we cannot have balance, duality and unity.

In hindsight, it was my own Cancerian nature that experienced the human condition very intensely and immediately. My awareness was never a curse; I could have ignored it and slowly gone mad or, even worse numb. If someone was pricking you in the leg, would you move or endure it. Pain is the messenger; sometimes, we don't move until we get the message. My pain was a prerequisite for change, an inconvenience that would shift my perception to love, not fear. Sometimes life brings us close when we are not truly fulfilled and without peace. Alan Watts said that we experience non-bliss to experience true bliss.

So how well can you transmute the duality individually and together? How do you move forward with less resistance? You cannot become mentally and spiritually strong if everything goes as planned without challenges and room for growth. I urge you to find meaning and learn about your extraordinary self. The meaning of life is your own creation, and it comes from the local destination, which is us. I learned that a happy person is not someone who ignores the bad and only deals with happiness. Someone who cannot integrate the opposite is not happy. Someone who can make peace and be calm is a useful person. Someone who reacts to their environment is destructive. We must centre ourselves before we do anything rash and clear your mind before reacting. I thank you for receiving my MESSage; know that you, too, can find the light in your own way and be able to help others through their mess then. If you wish to see this Universe, find the present moment, for it is where everything is happening. Uni meaning one, and verse meaning song.

"If you are intelligent and reasonable, you cannot be the product of a mechanical and meaningless Universe."
Alan Watts

MASON DAMIAN

Mason is a master of his own intuition using his playful approach to the Universe, he can balance a heavy burden with a soft disposition.

His perspective is strongly encompassed by Eastern Philosophy and practices and draws on natural law and therapeutic mindfulness that helps us return to our natural state.

He is a wise soul for twenty-one yet has attracted vast perspectives and experiences reaffirming that every individual has something special unfolding beyond most eyes. It's his calling to help others liberate themselves by sharing his story to spread hope.

Mason's story transmutes the suffering he experienced throughout his teenage years with mental health, where ultimately, he attempted suicide at eighteen years of age in 2019. His experience took him to his depths but also brought him copious amounts of knowledge and awareness. Eventually, after a psychedelic session, he had an awakening during meditation, and from there, he began to write what he had learnt.

Follow Mason's journey here:

https://www.instagram.com/masondamiannn/

THE ART OF AUTONOMY

T he creative arts are the keeper of authenticity. What you create, how you create and what you choose to create with are windows into a deeper layer of humanness. There is no place to hide in the creative process. You are in conversation with yourself with every decision you make. Play, doubt, confidence and the inner critic can all be found here, and anyone who has ever sat down, paintbrush or pen in hand, can attest to the duality of joy and frustration in creating art. From the moment the paint meets the canvas, your essence is imparted. There is an internal tug-of-war of self-doubt and curiosity that edges you forward to create, and it's somewhere here that the magic happens. The intimate relationship with the 'self' is unveiled, whether intentional or not and this vulnerability is infused in every mark. Every reaction, emotion and thought is reflected by so much more than the finished product. There is a depth that is unspoken and only felt. I could think of no better way to gently encounter the edges of your identity and experience of this world. This is Expressive Arts Therapy and the world Ipsarty curates for every client and this is my extraordinary.

I'm often asked, "what is arts therapy?" or met with preconceived ideas of what people think it is. Most people know the relaxing therapeutic benefits of art making, but few know its powerful role in therapy. Arts therapy is so much more than just creating art. The art itself acts as the third in the therapeutic relationship buffering some discomfort in sharing vulnerability. It helps to tell the story of its creator without the need for words. Every time we create, we place elements of ourselves into our creation, not for others to see or to analyse, but to witness ourselves. We can interact with ourselves this way while being safely held within the image, poem, song or play. Therein lies the power of arts therapy, respecting agency and the intuitive cues of readiness. At Ipsarty's core is the philosophy of agency, a person's fundamental right to be respected as the expert in their own lived experience. Ipsarty, the name of my business, comes from the word *ipseity*, which means self-hood and our sole focus is supporting the client to connect with their sense of self. In essence, our approach is based on giving autonomy and agency to the client and giving them a safely held space to process their world at their own pace. We empower them to problem solve, challenge inner stories with self-compassion, build confidence, connect with intuition, and find comfort within themselves. I've made it our mission to challenge the traditional modes of therapy and offer a new way of supporting people that recognises that there is no one size fits all approach. There is no single form of therapy that suits everyone.

Expressive Arts Therapy is therapy done differently. We don't conform to traditional ideals of therapist-led, solution-focused interventions. Because put frankly, there's nothing 'wrong' with any child or adult, and no one needs us to fix, improve or change them. The clients decide to transform the parts of their life if they choose, when, and how they choose to. We invite them to be exactly as they are and accept them in that season with open arms. Unfortunately, somewhere along the line, therapies subscribed to a deficit framework that seats professionals in the expert chair, while parents (and individuals) are expected to put aside their natural intuition and follow the 'expert' advice to the letter. Sadly, this therapeutic medical model approach leaves people disempowered and attached to the unachievable goal of 'perfection'. If you 'can't already tell, I have some passionate views about how professionals support people and even more so when it comes to children. It's time we stop sending the message to kids that they are not good enough the way they are. As a therapist I see these damaging messages seeping into the inner voice of our littlest souls and it is truly heartbreaking. The words that are said to them and even the ones that are implied become their inner narrative. It is our job as professionals to protect the sanctum of their developing sense of self, not dictate how they should fit into the world around them. The only disabling aspect of a disability is our culturally limiting attitude towards people's differences and autonomy. Where there is belief, self-belief grows.

I've learned this not only through my work as a therapist but on a much more personal level as a neurodivergent. My diagnosis of ADHD and SPD (Sensory Processing Disorder) announced itself at thirty years of age, after being informally diagnosed by a six-year-old client in the studio who pointed out I had "a brain like" hers while furiously scribbling her many busy thoughts in different coloured texters. She told me that her mind was like a busy shopping centre and as I looked at all those lines darting across the page in different directions, it dawned on me that she was right. My six-year-old ADHD/ASD client knew I was one of her people before I did. A few weeks later, I arrived at my official diagnosing appointment ten minutes late with no shoes because I forgot to put them on before leaving the house that morning (an embarrassingly common occurrence). Needless to say, all the evidence pointed to ADHD. Until then, I believed I was just a quirky, forgetful, clumsy, useless adult that shouldn't really be trusted in a kitchen. Looking back at my life with this new knowledge wasn't easy because the signs were always there, and I was left unsupported, feeling like there was "something wrong with me". This diagnostic label wasn't about medicalising my struggle or seeing myself from a deficit lens; it was the puzzle piece that always felt like it was missing in my identity. I remember the labels given to me as a child and the ones I gave myself. Lazy, unreliable, impulsive, reckless, stupid, sensititve, daydreamer, useless and the ever-present phrase of 'not living up to my potential.' Having this inner narrative caused havoc in my early adulthood with a string of traumas, as it does for many neurodivergent folk. But realising my brain was just processing the world differently quietened my inner self-critic and allowed space for genuine self-compassion. I finally knew how to begin supporting myself, and it started with finding the confidence to trust what felt right for me. If that means I hire a cleaner, or I have to use post-it notes all over my house to remind me to brush my teeth/hang washing out/drink water or have to keep a pair of spare shoes in the car in case I forget to wear them, then that's ok. I've learned to honour my unique rhythm and way of being. I also learned to celebrate the remarkable things my brain is capable of and how it views the world. I was always different, but finding my stride and wearing my uniqueness proudly, changed my life. We were never meant to be carbon copy humans; every difference shared with another enriches their life through the gift of widening perception. That one little six-year-old client gifted me this. It's funny just how much my professional work has impacted my life.

In all my years as a palliative, mental health, and disability nurse in the community, before training in psychotherapy, I have come to know that we can never truly understand what someone else's lived experience is. We can have all the theoretical knowledge in the world (thinking we know what's best for people) but genuinely miss the mark by thinking we are the experts. After years of witnessing the rawest side of being human, I have a humble appreciation for those who are brave enough to share their vulnerability with me. I've seen the immeasurable strength and love humans are capable of, and it changed me. Every patient/client changed me a little every day and continues to. There's one, however, that will forever stay with me and deserves a named place among these words, with his family's permission, of course.

Jamie Ellis was a firecracker, and when I cared for him, he was a palliative client with a neurodegenerative disorder ('Friedreich's ataxia) at nineteen years old, only a few years younger than me at the time. He had the most ferocious wit and equally matched temper. His dark humour was unlike any I've seen since, and he lived beyond the body that was failing him with his rebellious spirit. As his speech slowed and slurred more, and he lost the use of his hands, he never once allowed his autonomy to be taken away from him. He fiercely protected his right to choose and do the things he could. Jamie taught me the most valuable lesson as a professional; to witness and to really listen. Only a handful of people could understand him as he spoke in the later parts of his life, but it was here that I learned to listen with my whole body. Attune to the nuances of another person and observe more than just the words. He taught me how to take a back seat and hand the reins over even if the task would take an hour longer. This patience was more than just that; it was a form of honouring him as a person. His journey out of this world was difficult to witness at times as his own grief played out in front of me, but even as I grappled with the injustice of it, he taught me to accept that it is not my role to fix. I was forced to confront my discomfort in feeling helpless. On his worst days, he would be overcome by anger and lash out at everyone verbally and physically, which coined him the "behaviourally challenged client" label. Where others saw behaviour, I saw pain, anxiety, and a deep need to be seen. It was those days that he desperately needed the people he pushed away most. These lessons he gifted me helped me to carve out the therapist I am today, and I will be forever grateful that he graced this earth with his fiery presence. His tenacious value of autonomy was always in my mind as I designed our beautiful studio space.

The Ipsarty studio is truly an extension of who I am as a neurodivergent human and professional.

The foundations of our practice were laid by my lived experience of never quite feeling like I fit anywhere and the need for people to have a space to not only belong but just to be as they are. Somewhere they feel held and free from expectations. A place they can claim as their own for that short period of time that cradles them and softens the jagged edges of what they are experiencing in their life beyond our walls. When I set out to build my own therapeutic studio space, I envisioned it as a part of the therapy session, to come alive when someone entered the front door and to nurture them with its soothing energy. As professionals, we are quick to forget the potency of an environment on someone's mental landscape. And so, our studio beams with beautiful natural light and showcases my plant-buying addiction. It is a work of art that offers spaciousness. Walls are plastered with all manner of artwork to incite curiosity and inspire the creative soul in everyone. I designed every aspect of this space intentionally to support the needs of our clients; physically, energetically, emotionally, psychologically and on a sensory level. The environment sends gentle messages of safety and regulates those heightened nervous systems. It holds its own therapeutic presence without needing to "give therapy". Maybe my nursing origins influenced our holistic approach, but when we see each client as a whole, they begin to feel whole themselves.

So far, the studio lives up to my vision and is now a sanctuary for many clients (kids and adults alike). Much of our client base is neuro-divergent kids and their families navigating their way through their own diagnosis. And boy, do we get to witness some extraordinary families. Something magic happens when kids are given the green light on autonomy and agency. They begin to connect with who they are, and the more they learn about themselves, the more self-compassion they develop and the more confident they feel in communicating their needs and what feels right for them. They are supported to find their own rhythm and to learn to trust it. Kids need to be kids. They shouldn't feel pressured to live up to any therapist's expectations or goals. When they are given a chance to explore and process their world through play and their natural curiosity, they build skills from a base of empowerment and ownership over their own experience. Play, imagi-nation and creativity are how children process their inner and outer worlds, especially when words don't match their complex thoughts and feelings. Arts therapy moves what they are experiencing into a more fluid expression where any judgement of finding the right words or fear of being misunderstood is lifted through play. Through the arts, each child explores who they are, how they see themselves in their relationships, their environment and how they see themselves in the big wide world. And best of all, this happens how they choose and at the pace they need. We want to teach kids that this is ok and to lay the foundations for self-advocacy.

Our approach doesn't change from child to parent because the funda-mental aims are the same, connecting to identity, cultivating self-trust and replacing the inner negative narrative with self-compassion. The difference is that their patterns are often layered with guilt and shame that have been carried for many years. If I could wave a magic wand, I would wish for every parent of a disabled child to receive fully funded mental health support (and nourishing respite services). These parents are expected to shoulder too much alone. So many are merely surviving day by day and giving every ounce of themselves to nurturing their children and advocating for them. We choose to work closely with the whole family unit for this reason. Each child's parents are invited to engage in their own therapy or one of our parent support programs. With so many other professionals in their ears about what they should be doing, we focus our attention on boosting their confidence and trusting their instincts. This also extends into how they choose to support themselves.

So often, when we become parents, we shuffle ourselves to the side to meet the needs of our children first. And when burnout comes knocking at the door, everyone is quick to say you need to practise "self-care", and "take time out for yourself" with all the free time you have. Breathing exercises, meditation and exercise suggestions are printed on flyers and handed out as a bid to help regulate these fried nervous systems. While all of these options have their place, I want to acknowledge that when it comes to regulation, it can look as unique as the individual themselves. There are so many tools and strategies, but what works for one person may not work for another. Each of us holds our unconscious blueprint guided by our own sensory wisdom, the smells, textures, sights and sounds that comfort us. Sometimes we must be reminded that the "body" has a language of its own and carries an undeniable honesty in the human experience. Listening and attending to the little messages it is whispering takes practice and is something we often need to teach parents. Trusting the body and honouring its intuition after years of only valuing it for its pragmatic role requires a great deal of unlearning, but a regulated parent can coregulate a family. The incidence of carer burnout is staggering, and it's time that our wider community learns how to become the village these families so desperately need. Our reframe on 'self-care' is simply pausing with self-compassion in the micro-moments offered to us in everyday life. Children who see parents modelling self-compassion are far more likely to adopt this way of thinking for themselves. With my magic wand, I waved earlier; I'd also bestow this self-compassionate thinking onto every child. A generation of self-compassionate kids could change the world. But for now, we will concentrate on ensuring our mamas and papas know they are worthy and extraordinary and watch the ripple effect. And continue to encourage the inner artist in all parents and children.

The arts are a place of healing and transformation if chosen to be. As Expressive Arts Therapists, our role is to witness the humanness in another and meet that with our own authenticity. We aren't the guide; we are just the support crew. The lessons that have found me over years of journey alongside people have readjusted my professional identity and humbled my soul. To be seen and heard is everything but to amplify the autonomy of another is truly honouring the human in them. This is what Ipsarty is all about, and what an extraordinary privilege it is.

MEL WANGMANN

Mel Wangmann is a creative spark in the therapy world, offering a fresh approach to honouring the unique rhythm of every client through Expressive Arts Therapy.

She is the Founder and Director of Ipsarty, a one-of-a-kind arts therapy practice and neurodivergent sanctuary on the Sunshine Coast. Having spent over a decade nursing in the community, she encountered the tremendous healing power that creative arts can offer those seeking to be heard and seen. As a result, she was lured back to university to train in psychotherapy.

Being neurodivergent, she has developed her therapeutic approach using her lived experience to deliver holistic and nurturing mental health support to kids and families.

Mel is mama to baby Edie and bird mama to Butters the Eclectus Parrot/therapy parrot, who truly believes she's human.

Her potent voice as an advocate for neurodivergent folk can often be heard lecturing for universities and conferences, and on social media.

Follow along with her on:
Insta: @ipsarty
Website: www.ipsarty.com
Facebook: Ipsarty Arts Therapy

HAPPINESS IS DOWN SYNDROME

The night before everything changed, I sat in a dark theatre. There were forty high school students singing their hearts out to the show's final number. The costumes were spectacular, the production value was high, and the performers were right on their mark. But one girl stood out to me above all the rest. She had Down syndrome, and she had a spark about her. At that moment, I thought I was looking at her because I had never seen anyone like her in a play. Now I can say, wholeheartedly, that I was staring at my future.

The following day, 6th of March, 2020, I woke up bright and early to get ready. I regularly attended a women's Bible study, and on this particular day, I would be leading the entire group in worship. Being fourteen weeks pregnant and fresh on the heels of a miscarriage, I was immensely relieved and grateful that I had made it this far and was excited and hopeful. I remember feeling everything so deeply that day. Each hug and every kind word I heard felt like a soothing balm to my soul, and I couldn't stop the tears from flowing. Looking back, I can see that my mind, body, and soul sensed what was coming.

Shortly after arriving home, I threw off my boots, tossed on a hoodie, and curled under the sheets of my warm bed. My husband was working from home that afternoon, and my two-year-old son was napping, so it was the perfect opportunity to rest. I turned off the ringer on my phone and closed my eyes peacefully.

A minute later, I shot up in bed, looked at my phone, and saw a call coming through on silent. The caller ID said, 'B' I eagerly answered the call and jumped for joy. This was the call I'd been waiting for! Finally, I would learn the gender of my baby. With my first son, I'd held off on any genetic testing, but with THIS pregnancy, I was convinced I was having a girl and wanted confirmation so I could start shopping for cute baby clothes.

I squealed as I answered the phone. I'd waited weeks for these results, and it felt like Christmas morning. That is, until the doctor spoke.

Her tone was in stark contrast to mine. She was cold, far off, distant, and...scared? Hesitant? Worried? I couldn't quite pinpoint it, but I brushed it off as a clinical demeanour. She mentioned a few things about the NIPT test I'd been given and then uttered the sentence that is forever burned in my memory.

"Your test results came back as HIGH RISK for Trisomy 21."

This didn't quite compute in my brain. So, I asked, "What do you mean? Like...Down syndrome? What does high risk mean?"

"There is a 9/10 chance the fetus has Down syndrome," the doctor said.

From that moment on, it felt like I was underwater, gasping for air. Though my OB continued speaking, every word sounded muffled and difficult to understand. Then, finally, I heard her say, "do you have a piece of paper?" Though I was just steps away from my desk, I didn't think to go there. Instead, I pushed open my bedroom door and stumbled down the stairs. I saw a white, frilly doily from a party I'd thrown a week before, and I scribbled the number of a genetic counsellor who would help me better understand the results I was being given.

I was just about to hang up when I thought to ask, "what is the sex of the baby?"

"The fetus is a boy".

I threw down the phone, collapsed at the bottom of the stairs, and screamed like someone had been killed. I felt like the doctor told me I had six months to live, and there was nothing I could do. My husband rushed to my side, and I relayed all the information the doctor had given me between stifled sobs and heaving breaths. I wanted to escape from my body and mind.

"I cannot do this, Braden. This is NOT for me! I'm not this person! I can't do this!"

My usually soft-spoken, slow-to-speak husband said very clearly, "we can, and we will do this. This is our baby."

Had he not said those words with his firm love, had I been a single mother, had my parents or friends told me that my baby was not worth keeping, I'm not positive my amazing Jedidiah would be here today. Before those terrifying minutes at the bottom of the staircase, I would never, in a million years, considered not going through with a pregnancy. I believe strongly in the sanctity of life, yet this wave of terror felt like a beast, ready to trample my convictions and the fabric of who I am.

For an entire weekend, I did not get out of bed. I cried and slept on repeat. I prayed for the minutes, hours, and days to pass quickly until I met with the genetic counsellor. I desperately wanted answers, clarity, reassurance, and understanding. I desperately wanted.....something.

On Monday, 9 March, my husband and I met a genetic counsellor named Mara. We did not leave her office the same way we entered. God met us there in that boxed-in little cubicle, and I felt His hand on me as she spoke. She never once mentioned termination. She answered our questions clearly and calmly. She shared resources and support groups with us. She gave us statistics about siblings of children with Down syndrome and the positive impact they leave with them. Every bit of her speech was filled with hope and light.

I came home that day and poured into the resources she'd given me. I joined a support group of moms through the Down syndrome Diagnosis Network who were pregnant, like me, and considered "High risk" for Trisomy 21. I searched through the pages of my Bible, begging Jesus for hope. He delivered beyond my wildest imagination.

My gaze fell upon 2 Samuel 12:24-25. In this particular chapter, King David lost his son. In his grief, he WORSHIPPED God and went into his wife. They conceived another child and named him Solomon. An angel of the Lord was sent to rename him...Jedidiah. It means "Beloved of God." Tears of joy streamed down my face because I knew instantly that this would be my son's name. I knew and trusted wholeheartedly that my baby would not only be OK, but he was also BELOVED by God. I knew right then I'd been given a gift.

The months that followed that realisation were extremely difficult. The pandemic shut everything down just two weeks after I'd been given my potential diagnosis. I attended dozens and dozens of appointments without my husband. I stocked up on masks and sanitiser, terrified I would get the virus sweeping the world and potentially putting my unborn child at risk. I cried in parking lots, waiting for my appointments, while I blasted worship music in my car. One song became my anthem, and the chorus said:

"All my life, you have been faithful.
All my life, you have been so, so good.
With every breath that I am able
I will sing of the goodness of God."
("Goodness of God" by Bethel Music and Jenn Johnson)

Even when the future seemed so unclear and scary...Even when the shame of the feelings I experienced at the bottom of the stairs threatened to eat me alive... Even when it felt like my own body and emotions were working against this pregnancy...I could look back on other times in my life when God had been faithful and SING of the goodness of God. I could use the breath I'd been given to praise the God who was and IS ABLE and GOOD and JUST! I could worship the giver of all good gifts.

My most precious Jedidiah arrived, via emergency C-section, on 1st August 2020. The moment I saw him, I knew he had Down syndrome.

I also knew I didn't care. He was PERFECT, exactly the way he was created. My husband and I experienced a profound connection with him in the days following his birth.

The first spark was with me. I was wide awake in the middle of the night while my husband slept on a tiny couch next to my bed. The nurse brought Jed into our room for the first time since birth. I expected that he would be sound asleep like his daddy, but he wasn't. His eyes were wide open, and he didn't flinch as the nurse handed him to me. Instantly our eyes locked, and while streams of tears fell down my face, he stared into my soul. His beautiful, almond-shaped eyes communicated love and understanding. We had been through war together during my pregnancy, and he reminded me he was a fighter. He beat all the odds stacked against children like him in utero. He was letting me know that I was a fighter, too.

The next day, I sat in my bed reading some paperwork a nurse had brought to me, and I glanced up at my husband, holding Jedidiah. Tears were streaming down his face this time, and he said, "he's just staring at me." I told him about my experience the night before, and I knew the exact look he was talking about. Jed was magic, and we were the recipients of his wonder.

A few days after Jed was born, I was discharged, and he was admitted to the NICU for an infection that prevented him from eating. I will never forget the torment of leaving him behind. I was in great pain from my C-section, and yet, I would have walked twenty miles to get to him and deliver the milk I'd pumped at home. I cherished those hours I could hold him, skin to skin, even while hooked up to wires and machines. He was my precious miracle. He survived in my womb when the odds were stacked against him on every side. Yet, he was a WARRIOR and was so "beloved by God."

Jedidiah Coy Snyder came home on 8th August 2020 to an adoring big brother. Their initial moments together were like perfect poetry! As an only child who always longed for a sibling, their connection was the sweetest sight for me to behold. Those first few days and weeks together as a family of four were some of the best memories I've ever made. Of course, fear crept in every once in a while, as I learned a new term or was forced to find a different doctor or meet another early intervention therapist. But nothing ever came close to taking me back to those broken moments at the bottom of the staircase.

One night in October of 2020, just a few months after Jed came home, I jolted awake with a familiar song in my head. As a musical theatre actor, melodies regularly stream through the crevices of my mind. But this time, the tune was intricately interwoven with images of my newborn son. I started singing each line quietly not to wake anyone. The opening line of the song is,

"Happiness is finding a pencil. Knowing a secret, having such fun,"

I envisioned mothers of children like mine pushing their babies on a swing, feeding the ducks, dancing to music, and laughing with glee. I thought of my neighbour across the street who has an elementary-aged son with Down syndrome and pictured his sweet smile every time we passed his house. I felt like I was in on a secret, privy to only a few. The love and joy I felt while holding my boy was overwhelming, and I wanted to share that with anyone who would listen.

That moment was the catalyst for the birth of my third baby, "Happiness is Down syndrome." It's a place that exists on Facebook and Instagram for people like me, who question everything upon receiving a diagnosis. It's a place for community, honesty, and sharing. It's a one-stop shop to read stories, watch videos and look at pictures of individuals with Down syndrome and those who love them. I hope to reach those who have fallen through the cracks. Some mothers feel devastated by the prospect of having a life that has deviated from the plan they laid out, and I want to reach out and touch that mom. I want to say, "Just because your life is different from what you'd hoped does not make it a bad life. Many things about this life hold beautiful, hidden treasures the rest of the world will never get to taste and see.

I often describe the Down syndrome community as the secret garden you didn't know about and never wanted to find. It's usually covered in thick brush and thorny branches on the outside, but once you find the key, unlock the gate and step inside, overwhelming beauty is uncovered. The community is also like a bright orange, differently shaped shell hidden deep beneath the sand. You may have been looking for a white, perfectly shaped shell upon embarking on your sea adventure. But once this orange shell emerges from the sand, you are entranced by its effervescence and can't take your eyes off it. The white shell you were looking for initially is just as beautiful as it was before, but now you can see the nuance of this new shell.

Jed has changed my life for the better. Yet, I know I am still in the early days. He is only two years old, and I'm sure I have many difficult experiences ahead. But what stops me in my tracks is the overwhelming, life-altering joy I have found through being his mother. Though I switched doctors after that terrible phone call, I want to return to her and show off my amazing little boy. I want her to know how beloved he is by being him! But I don't ever want her or ANY doctor to impose their own biases or preconceived notions on a family like ours.

I want the world to know the truth about Down syndrome. The truth about Jed. He has a quality about him that is impossible to ignore. He loves life, and he truly sees people. When people cry, he cries. But when laughter fills a room, he smiles and enjoys the jubilee. Jedidiah knows how to make the most of every minute. He is not in a hurry, and he enjoys the view. Because of him, I can see pieces of myself I might never have discovered. He has opened up possibilities for my life. He has helped me spread my wings to fly.

This is a far cry from the woman I remember seeing at church as a child. I felt pity for her as she walked into the sanctuary, holding the hand of her disabled son. WHY? Why do so many of us automatically jump to a place of sadness when we see people who don't fit inside the box we have in our heads? What was the terror that consumed me when I received that call? On the other side, I can say it is not because Down syndrome is scary. The negative narrative surrounding Down syndrome has everything to do with the pressure and bogus expectations we put on ourselves and one another within society.

We strive to achieve success, accolades, wealth, adoration, and fame. We work so hard to keep up with the people around us, and we forget that most people around us are unhappy. Most people we encounter are not even close to leading rich, fulfilling lives. But you know who IS happy? My son with Down syndrome. And he's not alone. Statistically, 98% of people with Down syndrome are happy with who they are. They love life. They love people. They love themselves.

And why shouldn't they? They are living, breathing, wonderful people made in the image of God! Just like you and me. Our worth and value should not be placed on our accomplishments, looks, wealth, or other grand endeavours. Our worth lies in the hands of the Father. He says we are worthy. He says we are loved. The striving for perfection can cease because God is perfect. We can rest easy knowing we are all right where we should be. I can sleep soundly tonight, knowing I'm doing the exact thing I was put on this planet to do.

Jed is my mission. People are my mission. Love is my mission.

I have so much to be grateful for. I barely recognise the person who was crying at the bottom of the stairs. That woman has walked through some deep and rocky waters and is not the same. Yet, by God's grace, she chose to stand up, wipe the tears and take tiny baby steps forward to the new chapter of her life. And here I am, writing this chapter in this book. I can't wait to see what comes next...

MISTY COY SNYDER

Misty Coy Snyder is an actor, writer, singer, worship leader, content creator and disability advocate.

She lives with her husband Braden, and their two sons, Clay and Jedidiah, on the East Coast. Before Misty embarked on her advocacy journey, she spent her days performing around the world.

Her passion for connecting, building community and opening up the door for communication has been growing in her since she was a little girl doing community theatre and a local radio show with her mother. So, when Jed was born in August of 2020, she channeled all of her training on and off stage to spread the good news of Down syndrome. She wants NO ONE to feel alone in this journey but rather feel loved and seen.

You can find her advocating daily on: @happinessisdownsyndrome and @mistycoysnyder. If you reach out to her through one of these platforms, she will respond with joy.

FINDING THE RIGHT ROAD TO MY SON'S VILLAGE

2007 was the year my world changed. I didn't know it then, but I do now. It was the year my special son arrived.

He is the youngest of five boys, the second time I had to leave my hometown to deliver. His birth was the hardest of them all. Harder than my first and harder than my third, who came into this world on the front seat of a commodore. Little did I know he was telling me something from the beginning.

I want to be here and enjoy what the world has to offer, but I don't do things easily.

My boy was a very contented and happy baby, but he didn't meet milestones. I sought advice when he was eighteen months old. In my remote country town, our visiting paediatrician gave

a diagnosis of developmental delay and ruled out ASD as he had excellent eye contact. Following the diagnosis, we walked a path through the government health system. Their allied health service provided visiting speech and occupational therapists, who flew into town. This system changed staff regularly and without notice. The booking system was unorganised, and they were predominantly trained in aged care. These healthcare providers supported children and young people but did not specialise in my son's needs.

We soon discovered that my son's development was severely delayed, he wasn't improving after regular therapy sessions, and he would need a lot of extra support/appointments. So it was recommended we obtain both mental health and chronic disease plans. An incredible doctor organised his first plan, which went for twelve months. After that, all seemed to be going reasonably smoothly. We were on the road of our public health system, one which would guide and support us both to give my son the best opportunities for development.

How wrong was I? I was unaware of how difficult the road ahead was going to be. Growing up in the country, touring around was a regular occurrence. Whether going for a Sunday drive to the beach for a fish, out behind the dog fence for a BBQ or travelling to the city for appoint-ments or holidays, we were always prepared for the trip. However, this trip was different. I was not prepared at all for our journey ahead.

In my hometown, the medical industry was fluid, doctors changed regularly, and often they were unfamiliar with our Medicare system. I had to go in batting from the very early days to advocate for my son to have his health plans renewed. Once, when I rang Medicare to ask questions, the lady said to me, "and who are you?' I replied, "mum of my special son." She replied, "these are questions a doctor would usually ask, not a parent." I said "yes, but my son's doctor doesn't know our Medicare system, so I need to learn as I am trying to educate them for my son to receive the support he needs."

I always appreciated the services we were provided and felt grateful to the specialists who travelled so far and were there for us, so when I wanted to get a second opinion, I felt a sense of betrayal to them. The GP assured me this was ok and something they supported as they had seen my son's difficulty in the community. This led to a diagnosis of Autism Spectrum Disorder (ASD). I have always accepted my son's ASD diagnosis, although he has never fitted it well. It brought me to intersections which gave me direction to learn different ways of teaching.

I travelled for workshops, for knowledge of information, and to meet people with experience. I attended the APAC in 2013 and helped organise Positive Partnership to hold a workshop in our hometown to help educate and bring awareness of Autism to our community.

These early struggles which caused conflict between myself; a mum, and professionals, was preparing me for the bigger picture of a child with a disability in our system. I had to harden up, and I had to stay focused. I had to find the inner strength to keep consistent and strive for the best support my son needed. Our experience showed us the systems are not suitable for everyone, and sometimes you have to go your own way and take things into your own hands.

Attending school became unrealistic. We were approved part-time but soon after, we felt pressure to be full-time. He wasn't coping with part-time, was not fully toilet trained, had no attention to task, no communication, and found fine and gross motor very challenging. Home-schooling quickly became the best option; having to privately employ staff to accommodate his needs and become a program manager myself, without training, also learning how to make and where to find resources. All of this consumed every spare moment I had. When I wasn't doing business bookwork, attending to my other children, making resources, or planning, I would worry about him. Am I doing the right thing? How can I help him learn? How do I find out what I don't know? I am not a reader, and I am not a googler. I am not a highly educated woman. I am a mum. I am a wife. I am me.

Through this, I learnt to take things one step at a time with advice from someone here or someone there, someone within the education system or health system, or someone who knows someone or heard of something. I became more proactive, enquiring about this therapy and that therapy, trialling many different ideas. I was eclectic, struggling to stick to one way. What shone through was Applied Behaviour Analysis, proving the most effective and the hardest to implement. It became the choice of therapy. Gradually he was learning, out of nappies, feeding himself, showing some interest in playing, learning to move in the water, building skills and developing in the slowest ways, but developing!

With the mutual parting of a couple of very special ladies teaching my son, I attempted to take this role on as well. Disaster hit! I was Mum to five children, my husband worked away Monday to Friday, and I was a full-time carer and teacher of a special child. I crashed!!

At the time, I was advised no therapy was better than bad therapy. I rested on this. We were losing a lot of information he had learnt in a short time. His behaviour became unmanageable. I was isolated in a very small town. It was tough! But I had no choice but to move forward. Having become a reader and googler, I began searching for schools and supports in our capital city. This became obsessive with so many options I was driving blindfolded. I had no idea where the best destination was, or any idea which track to take. My husband and mum thought moving to a large regional town would be a great start. "Try it for twelve months." was my husband's suggestion. The decision to move to this large regional town was an excellent one. It was a beautiful location closer to our hometown than the city, and only a four-hour drive to get back home or for my husband to visit. This town has lots of great support and fun things to do. It has the highlights a city offer, all within a five minute drive. A cinema, a theatre, an indoor pool, and private therapists who are dedicated to their businesses and provide a personal and professional service. The ocean, great food, familiar faces, a great mix of country and city life.

The move was enormous. Our first son had just returned from overseas and was settling down in the city at university and work. Our second son had just finished year twelve and went straight into university. Our third son was moving to boarding school and our fourth was staying at home with his dad, who returned to live permanently. My husband had not lived and worked in our hometown for at least fourteen years, only ever coming home for weekends or holidays. He is a dedicated provider for us all.

2017 was a big year for our family. First, our two eldest settled into the real world of living together, working and studying. Then, my special son and I settled into a new town and home, and my third son moved into boarding school alone. Finally, my husband and fourth son stayed at our family home. I could not have predicted this is what my family would look like. 2017 was my hardest year ever.

This relocation was born out of necessity, I hadn't thought a lot about how I would cope or even if I would cope. I had to do something to help my son, so I had to try it. I learnt to support our family business from 400km away and arrange support for our son in our new home. Looking back, I am unsure how I managed all of this. I know I didn't at times. My mum has always been my rock and a fantastic role model to stand up for what is right and always support the family even if it's hard. My husband and other children were incredible, never questioning me and my passion for giving our special son and brother the best opportunity in life.

Taking the risk of venturing out of our comfort zone to offer a better life for our son was paying off. Slowly he became more manageable, thanks to a dedicated ABA therapist. Within three months of our move, my mum told me, "He is improving, I can see the change in him." My life was very restricted. There was no socialising. No time for myself. I only did work for the business and work for my son – making resources and learning the rules of ABA. We didn't do any eclectic therapies, just ABA. It was extremely tough but so rewarding to think we were finally making change for him to become the best he could be. He is learning to control his impulsive negative behaviours. Learning socially acceptable behaviours. Learning to build his desire to want to do things. It is allowing him to experience activities neurotypical children have.

These past five years have not been easy. At times it has put stress on our marriage and family I could not have envisaged. I was ok to give up my life to help him have the best one he could have. I didn't want the rest of the family to have to give up theirs. I now know they did have to give up part of their life for him, as they had to give me up. They had to give up their mum and dad living together; they had to give up time with us as a whole family. I wasn't there for them as I should have been. As I wanted to be. They have proven to be exceptionally extraordinary brothers and sons to continue living their best lives amidst the different format of our family.

Pre-pandemic, my son's paediatrician asked if I was interested in doing some more genetic testing. It had been ten years, and new testing is evolving all the time; Having four older brothers, it would be nice to know if genetics played a role in his condition, considering they are becoming an age they may wish for a family themselves. I agreed it was a good idea. Eighteen months after our appointment with the geneticist, we received a result of stxbp1. Wow!! The geneticist rang me and described the characteristic, which gave me instant excitement and the tears started flowing. She was able to describe him to a tee. It fitted!

A lady who had only met him once was able to describe him so accurately; sure; it wasn't exact, like Autism; there is a spectrum, some have this, some don't, others do this, and others don't. The exciting thing is he finally has a diagnosis that suits him. One which was right. There was also a bonus, it wasn't inherited from my husband or myself, and the chances of his brothers fathering a stxer is the same as anyone else. Mixed emotions followed the initial phone call. While he did not experience seizures like a high percentage of stxers, the outlook on ability and communication was disheartening. There is lots of talk about regression during and after adolescence. Some children are unable to walk or talk. Stxbp1 undoubtedly has challenges. The upside, some can run, jump and talk, read and ride bikes, some can express themselves, and some can even study. Stxers love social interaction, love to be around people and, especially, family. They have unconditional love for living and waking up to a new day. My son is the epitome of this. He is an inspiration to learn from. Each day is a new day. Each day is a day worth exploring. Each day you can wake up and wonder what you will learn today, what will come your way today, and who you will see today. Each day you can feel excited and satisfied.

My second son is now living in Holland for a few months. As I write this, I can't help but think about "Welcome to Holland", a prominent and well-known essay written by American author and social activist Emily Perl Kingsley about having a child with a disability. It was very early after my son's diagnosis. I was grieving. Our family has experienced both Holland and Italy, and we have adapted and enjoyed what both offer. Both have brought us happy and sad times. Both have proven to be fun, loving and joyful. Both have been fulfilling and memorable. It is hard to imagine what life would be like if we never visited Holland.

Since the diagnosis of stxbp1, I am finally enjoying what Holland offers. I am learning about tulips and windmills. I realise my grief and pain are going, and peace is prevailing. Peace with myself that I have done the best at the time with the knowledge I had. The peace that my son didn't learn how our health system advised me. Peace, I made the right decision to question professionals. Peace, I do things differently, but I am not alone. Peace, my son is a minority. Being at peace is now allowing hope to build, allowing our lives to be freer. Peace gives us time to reflect on all the extraordinary angels my special son has brought into our lives. Peace at where I am now, which is allowing me time to stop and think, reflect, time for me to regencrate, restore, refocus, and renew my desire to dream again.

Learning the importance of surrounding ourselves with the right people has made our journey exciting. People who are strong and genuine, who strive for the best in themselves and who aren't afraid of differences. From the beginning, he has had various small villages support him, showing kindness and understanding, showing a caring nature to guide him forward. At present, my son has a fantastic large village around him. The biggest one he has had his whole life. One who knows the community laws, what is expected of him and how they can support him to be the best he can be. They are bringing him forward, showing him what he is capable of and only accepting the best he has to offer.

My family have become extraordinary humans because of this long twisted rough road our special son has directed us down. We have experienced extraordinary staff who have been drawn to him, whether they are regulars in our home for therapy or see him once a week in the community. Extraordinary strangers attend to him on an air flight or help him at the supermarket or allow him to attend mainstream learning opportunities, such as an art class or a public swimming session. Extraordinary angels, I thank you! I thank you for treating our son and brother with respect and kindness, treating him the same as others, and allowing him learning opportunities in which he rises to the occasion. These opportunities allow him to prove that he can achieve great things. They show him he can be like the others. I am at peace that the road had to be rough and bumpy. I had to lose the map and get lost several times, and my car even had to break down. At peace, this had to be the way in order to find the smooth, newly bituminised surface. One which allows us to go a little faster now and has some clearer signage. This road may still bear unplanned detours or traffic jams, but I am ready for this part of the journey. I'm learning how to bypass certain places which find differences hard to accept and learning to see the fast lane to those who bring out the best in my son.

Our journey still has a long way to go, and we are better prepared. Prepared not to give up when a system is not right. I understand it is healthy to question and follow strong beliefs, and my intuition is paramount to continue finding the best support for our son. Our extraordinary son and brother have brought us an extraordinary life and has made us extraordinary people. He has attracted extraordinary angels who have shown us how strangers can become such an integral part of our lives. They, like my son, show unconditional love and passion for humankind. One I had not experienced before. One I will always be forever grateful.

NICHOLE DUREGON

Nichole is one of those women who hold themselves with Grace and humility but also knows when to armour up and hold the line, especially when it comes to justice for the underestimated.

She is a mother of five boys, a business owner, and a wife who has had to live away from her husband and family home for five years to seek the best medical support for her son with special needs. She is a fierce and courageous advocate for families, especially those like hers, finding their way through a broken system.

Nichole has spent years advocating for and questioning the systems in her local area for her son and others with special needs to live the life they deserve. Having to fight her way, and choose a new adventure for her extraordinary son, has shown Nichole, not just how dysfunctional some of the systems are but just how truly remarkable some humans can be.

She lives in South Australia with her youngest son, spending weekends at her family home with her husband. Her four older boys are out of school living wonderful lives working, travelling and at university. She adores her family, and even though theirs isn't the usual dynamic, she wouldn't change their extraordinary for the world.

SUPERPOWERS

The way we interact with the world as humans is quite fascinating because we're all unique and quirky in our own way. With the behavioural observations of young children these days, thanks to advanced research and a dedicated focus on the topic, we are thankfully able to help young ones navigate through life with support, education and an understanding of what makes them special. We're lucky to have an abundance of tools, resources and educated professionals helping us navigate the complexities of the body and brain to enable the growth and development of successful adults in years to come.

While it can be a tricky journey to navigate, coupled with geographical challenges in accessing professionals in the fields we need, it's worth pursuing, nevertheless.

After consultation with friends and family, I find that quite often, when we as adults and parents or carers are working through the diagnosis passage with our child/ren, we start to answer for ourselves, the responses that generate an ASD, ADHD or sensory diagnosis. Of course, many assessments are completed and reviewed in parallel to each other; however, on the surface, 'tick, tick, tick' begins to become the voice in our heads as we jump to conclusions and diagnose ourselves with no qualification to do so.

It's important to realise that there are degree-qualified professionals for a reason and that education, explanation, balance and perspective are essential.

When it comes to tasks, it can be done if I give myself one hour to do something. If I give myself two hours, it'll take the entire two hours. So, if I had twenty nine years, six months and five days to do an assignment, I'd start it in twenty nine years, six months and four days.

Without self-awareness, learned behaviours and observed practices, including a solid plan, deadlines to meet, goals set with clear objectives and actions mapped out, the land of the drifter would invade.

In the time set aside to write, I have eaten Nutella straight out of the jar, responded to messages and emails, and posted to a community Facebook page. I have reviewed the analytics of my websites, and spoken to my Dad and then my brother on the phone – I made both calls! I have put clothes in the washing machine and checked on my dog. All these things did not need to happen in the time dedicated to writing.

I find this amusing and interesting all at the same time. I know I have a short attention span coupled with an ability to hyperfocus, I can work at a million miles an hour and be disciplined during that hyperfocus period. It comes back to my earlier point, though, without a solid plan, deadlines, goals, objectives, lists and a map, it won't get done. But I know how to leverage these odd quirks to my advantage.

I have taken many online tests in an attempt to label myself and my quirks; however, that's about as far as I've taken it. I don't need to tick a box or have a label to know and leverage my uniqueness.

When it comes to children, though, that's another story.

When my son was six years old, we also discovered he had some quirks. Quirks that required early intervention to enable him to live his best life while navigating this world with a brain that thinks quite differently from most others. At the same time, for the following few years, , my eldest daughter would face the same challenges; however, she would successfully hide these and morph, chameleon style, to suit her surroundings, mimicking perceived 'normal' behaviours and therefore not raising any flags.

When Alan started kindy in 2013, his teachers began sharing concerns with me just one month after commencing. As a result, in the March of 2013, a two-page report with a timeline of incidents was presented, intended to aid a discussion with our General Practitioner to initiate the investigation process.

After speaking with Alan's wonderful former carer from family day care, she confirmed she had not witnessed the behaviours outlined in the report that the kindy had provided. Alan was much loved in his family-focused and small family day care setting, and it's obvious now, in hindsight, why the traits he began demonstrating in Kindy hadn't been observed before this time.

Alan's family day care environment was filled with love, care and a small group of three children in a family home. He then entered a kindergarten room with twenty-something other young children and just two teachers. The sensory overload he experienced every day of his five-day fortnight was upsetting, albeit we didn't know this at the time.

After consultation with our General Practitioner and the perspective of Alan's family day care carer, we decided to see how the first few months of Kindy went before proceeding down the investigative path.

In the June of his Kindy year, another letter came home from the school requesting further information, assessments and support.

Over the following few months ,Alan was assessed by an Occupational Therapist, Speech Therapist, Hearing Specialist, Paediatrician and Psychologist. They recommended therapy; however, no one could give a clear diagnosis yet. Alan completed his kindy and prep year and received a great result for his readiness screening in preparation to transition to year one.

Alan moved to a new school for year one and had two incredible teachers. Gifted and caring, they were the dream teachers you want for your child. However, in this new environment and with fresh eyes, the flags raised again, and another set of assessments were requested. It was now 2015, and we were two years into this journey with our six-year-old.

Towards the end of 2015 and the start of 2016, with new reports, assessments and results, many recommended that a diagnosis was now warranted. So began, our rapid race to capture early intervention funding before Alan turned seven in the April of 2016.

Handwritten, on a Paediatricians letterhead dated 24 February 2016, read the words, "High functioning autistic disorder with significant sensory issues, anxiety and attention difficulties."

With that letter, I had less than six weeks to access whatever funding was available for early intervention, something I recognise now, in hindsight, that we should have had from 2013 when he was four.

Every specialist, therapist and doctor who assisted us on this journey bent over backwards to support and help. We jumped queues, were seen by Autism Queensland quite quickly and obtained some pre-paid therapy and a handful of sensory resources we could use for years to come.

I wanted to set my son up for success. But I knew the road ahead would be challenging without the proper support structure, thanks to my best friend, Christina, who had a daughter quite a few years older than Alan and who had Asperger's Syndrome.

Our journey with NDIS (National Disability Insurance Scheme) was a long and challenging one which commenced in 2018 after we'd spent five years funding therapy and assessments as a family. Again, it was our General Practitioners' suggestion to seek help, and once again, I found myself on a path of navigating red tape and ducking and weaving through rules and conditions. Even though there is a strong desire not to limit my son in life, on paper, I had to show how he would be severely limited in life without support.

Navigating the NDIS process was one of the most heartbreaking, confusing and soul-destroying challenges I've ever had to steer. Initially, we were declined for support, but we, requested a review, gathered additional evidence, and were eventually approved for a low-level funding scheme to support the necessary therapy. Unfortunately, this meant the path to crafting a contributing adult member of society, was beyond what our family budget could accommodate.

Medication was not the answer for Alan, even though it was trialled. Instead, we found other ways to help him navigate this world and regulate himself through communication techniques, learned behaviours, essential oils and diet.

While Alan is acutely aware of his uniqueness, he hasn't yet realised how extraordinary his gifts are.

I am in awe of how my children think and approach this world. The way they tackle challenges, tasks and curiosities. The way they learn when they make mistakes, pull themselves up and embrace their authentic selves. Yes, some things need to be taught and practised before becoming a 'normal' habitual behaviour, but that is what intervention and therapy are for, after all.

In 2020 my chameleon of a daughter, Madison, began displaying traits similar to that of someone living with high-functioning autistic disorder and attention difficulties. I knew how common it was for girls to be diagnosed much later in life than boys, thanks to their ability to mimic behaviours and what they perceived as 'normal'. What I hadn't accounted for was that it would happen under my own roof, given my awareness and experiences thanks to my best friend, Christina.

It wasn't my first rodeo this time, and I was prepared to go all in and do what it took to get the understanding, awareness and support for Madison that Alan had been privileged to receive for so long.

It's a very different journey to travel with a young woman in her final years of high school, with a level of maturity most can only hope to observe in their teenage daughter. Yet, with a demonstrated sense of social justice and strength, Madison's ability to fly under the radar was remarkable upon reflection.

Throughout the journey, which was prompted by an evident failure to mimic expected behaviours, Madison continues to excel, albeit while learning about herself and how she works simultaneously. Talented in what I like to label 'street smarts' and with a love of any history subject, Madison is exceptionally gifted in her thinking and awareness of the world and how it works.

Perhaps the pandemic had something to do with this unravelling? After all, there were no face-to-face friends her age to mimic anymore.

It must be a teenage trait because, like Alan, Madison, too, does not realise how special she is and that the world is simply waiting for an extraordinary person like her.

While with each opportunity presented initially by a challenge, I can learn much from hindsight. With time comes experience and under-standing, and many 'what ifs' can come to mind. It's essential to focus on what you can do as a parent or carer right now, not what you can't do, might have missed or should have done. Your power as a parent or carer is that of self-control. You can't control what is happening to you or around you, but you can control how you react —controlling your response, how you handle a situation and regu-lating yourself.

While it's never going to be an easy journey; you need to give yourself a break, not be too hard on yourself and definitely, and don't take yourself too seriously. This journey of life is a marathon, not a sprint.

Having been on this trek of observing the navigation of life while thinking differently from most for quite some time now, the more I've learnt, observed, witnessed, tested, trialled and sought advice, the more I realise how quirky we all are. I know there are labels we need to define to understand our ways of operating in this world and, of course, for funding and support purposes. But what I have noticed the most is just how much of a superpower it can be when you fit the box for High-Functioning Autism Spectrum Disorder (ASD) or Attention Deficit Hyperactivity Disorder (ADHD).

I keep telling my children that they have a superpower within them. As soon as they figure out how to truly leverage it to their advantage and embrace it, the world will be waiting for them and the gifts they bring. Notwithstanding the amazingness they pose right now, of course.

ADHD superpowers for some include high energy, hyperfocus, resilience building, creativity cultivation, conversational skills, spontaneity and courage, to name a few. It can bring out-of-the-box thinking, humour, drive and the passion that comes with it for projects and activities. It can mean having a seemingly endless amount of energy that you're able to channel towards success and goals.

A trademark of the condition is the ability to hyperfocus. Many people grow to be active and involved adults who have successful careers with ADHD due to their ability to focus on what they're doing for hours on end. Some also can push past setbacks and have an immense amount of resilience, adapting to new strategies, ideas and thoughts to troubleshoot solutions to complex problems.

The attention deficit component doesn't always mean a lack of attention. It can mean paying attention to everything, especially things many others will miss. Couple this with sensory processing challenges, and the overwhelm can be enormous.

While this is only one perspective of ADHD and isn't a one-size-fits-all outfit for all, it is evident how knowing this condition, knowing yourself and leveraging both to your advantage can result in incredible output.

High-functioning Autism Spectrum Disorder superpowers include attention to detail, deep focus, observation skills, systematic and novel approaches, integrity, tenacity and resilience, acceptance of differences and visual skills, to name a few.

Unfortunately, the familiar words you'll hear or read when high-functioning Autism Spectrum Disorder is discussed or written about are words like deficit, rigid, delayed and not flexible, as a few examples. However, what most don't realise is how much of a blessing it can indeed be when you have a diagnosis like this and can support someone to align their life and goals by working with the gifts they've been given.

Most children are creative and have an imagination we can only dream of re-experiencing. Creativity 't limited to play, though; one of the outstanding traits of a child with high-functioning ASD is creative thinking.

Imagine the problems of the world we could solve with the creative thinkers who pay attention to detail, can focus immensely, notice things others don't and work methodically with integrity, honesty and resilience.

Attention Deficit Hyperactivity Disorder and High-Functioning Autistic Disorder are genuine superpowers. Through education and awareness, we can enable an environment to thrive.

"Extraordinary children with special gifts and vulnerabilities have a great purpose. They aren't their diagnosis, and they aren't their label. They are not more than or too much. They don't have to be limited by the confines of the traditional medical or societal system. They hold limitless joy. They have the capacity to share limitless love. They are extraordinary".

NYREE JOHNSON

Nyree Johnson is a passionate advocate for diversity and equality, focused on empowering and supporting her community.

She is an an avid writer and published author. Outside of her writing life, Nyree is an award-winning small business owner and a dedicated community volunteer. She writes and works to instil and inspire confidence, promote resilience and enable success to the people who surround her.

Nyree also has a fulfilling corporate career and lives in Queensland, Australia with her husband, Nathan, and their three children.

Living an Intentionally Imbalanced life, you will find Nyree loving life, doing what she loves, ensuring she is always exactly where she wants to be.

To connect with Nyree, find her social links on:

www.nyreejohnson.com.au

EVIE'S AWESOMENESS

"What's wrong with your child?" the stranger asked, pointing a finger in Evie's face. They weren't even looking her way. "What's wrong with her"?

I sighed. *Here we go again,* I thought. I was used to this question, and after numbing myself appropriately, I took a deep breath and replied in a robotic monotone:

"Well, she has Partial Trisomy 9 and Partial Monosomy 6, and she has multiple ventricular septal defects, and she can't walk, and she can't talk, and she has Laryngomalacia, and respiratory issues…" I trailed off, finishing my spiel weakly, eyes already searching for an escape route.

The stranger was lost. She looked bored and uncaring. A chasm of fear and indifference opened between us. She nodded a bit and then walked off, widening the chasm. It could swallow me whole. *At least she didn't say that she knows how it feels,* I thought. I might have snapped if she did.

But as she walked away, the relief I felt for it to be over quickly turned to anger and frustration.

Why must I keep answering this stupid question? Why do I even bother with strangers who clearly don't care or even try to understand? So often, it was just easier to stay home, in a safe bubble: just me and my beautiful daughter Evie.

Evie was two years old by this time, so I'd had two years of fielding these questions. And when there weren't questions, there was just... staring. Staring and fear and judgement. Two years of all that, on top of my own fear, grief, panic, and the daily uncertainty of being a mother to a super rare child.

I remember the doctors' first words to describe Evie when she was born.

"She has a very rare chromosome mutation that's incompatible with life," they said. *Incompatible with life.*

"Your daughter has congenital defects, skeletal abnormalities, and dysmorphic features, and she is failing to thrive. If she survives, which isn't likely, she will have severe mental retardation."

They were just words, but I felt their weight. Crushing. Devastating. Beyond their literal meaning, they added painful wounds to a conversation filled with terror and fear. These words held within them their own trauma.

Incompatible. Defective. Dysmorphic. Abnormal. Retarded. Mutated. Failure.

To me, Evie was none of those things. She had never been anything but freedom and love. Evie was a new soul in the world – fragile, but beautiful and full of potential. Like all of ours, her birthright was love, support, acceptance and inclusion. Yet, none of the words I was told spoke into her uniqueness, her spirit, or her humanity.

This diagnosis language has become so ingrained in our vernacular, so overbearing, that we all speak it fluently now and all fall into the habit of medicalising our children. These words steal potential and ability. They trap us in the thinking that *this is the only language we get to speak* around our children.

It wasn't long after that last "what's wrong with her" conversation that I experienced a monumental shift in how I approached language. It was the day I discovered that Evie had superpowers.

--

In New Zealand, there is a piece of open road between Christchurch and Timaru that we would drive along to visit family. On a particular part, there are electrical pylons that we would drive under, and the strangest thing would happen when we did. Every time, as we got closer to this patch of road, Evie would start crying. Out of nowhere, she would start up, even if it was dark, even if she was asleep. We'd drive under the pylons, and she would wake up and cry, and then when we passed them, she'd stop and go back to sleep. It happened so often; it became a thing. I tried my best to understand what could cause this phenomenon, and all I could come up with was that she must have an electromagnetic sensitivity: she feels something, and she doesn't like it. I realised it also happened in supermarkets and any time we passed through electric sliding doors. So she had some kind of sensitivity around magnetic and electric fields.

This phenomenon got me excited. Like, really excited. Because to me, this just proved that she was magic. So I started saying that she had superpowers, as a light-hearted way to describe it. She was like a baby Magneto, from X-Men.

Over time, this idea about superpowers grew into something incredibly profound. I thought deeply about Evie and all the things she was teaching me and those around her. I thought about the things that made her unique: her character, personality, and the things she could do. She evoked a level of care and love from people they'd never experienced. She had a fragility and pure joy that drew people towards her. She loved being on a beanbag and always had the most delicious laugh when we played with her on one. She loved to splash about in the water and wriggle up and down a couch on her back. She was mischievous and funny, charming, and delightful. She allowed us to throw away the charts, rules, structures, and expectations. We lived in freedom in each moment. She was a pure presence.

This awareness of my own thinking about Evie shifted how I spoke about her. I was so tired of people only seeing things that were 'wrong' with my daughter – their negative framing of difference was their first observation of her.

So, armed with this new language, my new way of describing her, I was ready for the questions. It wasn't long before someone again asked me: "What's wrong with her?"

This time I smiled, and replied cheekily, "Nothing. Nothing is wrong with her. In fact, she has superpowers!

The stranger looked at me oddly. "What do you mean?"

And just like that, I got to reframe the whole conversation, and steer it toward ability, uniqueness, joy, hope and love. I shared the things I adored about Evie and talked about the things she loved. I shared stories and snippets of our life, her character, and her two-and-a-half-year-old gorgeousness. They looked at Evie then and told me how beautiful she was. "Oh, what deep sparkly eyes she has! And such delicate fingers!"

At that moment, because I had described a human being, they saw a human being. Instead of a collection of failing body parts, and big words to be afraid of. I shared humanity, they saw it, embraced it, and leaned into it. When they walked away, there was no chasm of fear and indifference. Instead, we had built a bridge over difference, and called it acceptance, inclusion, and belonging.

Now I loved being able to share things about my child, and I wanted to be asked about her. But so many questions we ask each other seem to default to clichés. We ask things like, "How old are they? Are they walking yet? Are they talking yet? Do they sleep through the night? Are they eating solid food yet?" We are asking, pershaps subconsciously, "are they normal?"

Which to me seems like a very boring question. For Evie, it's entirely useless.

Normal? What is normal??

We ask so many performance-based questions. In fact, we ask perfor-mance-based questions as soon as the tiniest spec of humanity is on a scan. We measure, prod, weigh, evaluate and conclude the value of a child before that child is even born. And then, after birth, it continues. We are measuring, prodding, weighing, evaluating, making new conclusions, and more measuring.

There are so many forms from Growth Charts to NDIS forms to Needs Assessment Documents. I must have completed every one of them over Evie's life, most of them more than once.

One day, I hit a wall while filling in yet another form. Or a wave or something. It was a deep despairing sadness. I was asked to tick boxes that would indicate my child's abilities, and I couldn't tick a single question. On a two-page form, I couldn't say yes to anything. Evie couldn't do the 'typical' two-year-old activities and had barely met a few of the 3-month-old milestones. It felt so hopeless.

Ironically these forms are designed to help. They can paint a picture of where funding, support and assistance need to be delivered. So, my empty form would clearly indicate that we had some room for assistance.

But as a parent, to get this assistance, we're constantly forced to paint such a negative picture of our child. We must share the deficits; the *can't do*s, and the *no ticks* in the boxes. We're encouraged to list all the "bad things" - everything about our child is medicalised and dehu-manised. It wears us down, hurts our hearts and breaks our spirit.

And so, I broke.

All the negativity, judgement, fear and uncertainty overwhelmed me. I hated this form. I hated all the forms. I hated having to fill them in, I hated the dumb questions, I hated that the person receiving my docu-ment-with-no-ticks would think that Evie was a blob who couldn't do anything, that she cost the system money, that she was *a nothing*.

I just wanted the person at the other end to see the value in Evie, how many abilities she had and how much I loved her. But nothing on this document allowed Evie's humanity to be present. I wanted to be asked about the things Evie *could* do. She wasn't a blob, and she wasn't nothing. Evie was worth every penny of care and support.

So, I decided to make up my own form, to go alongside the official one, with much better questions. I considered all the things Evie enjoyed doing, everything she could do, and I created questions that I could already answer *YES* to. I called this new form "Evie's Awesomeness!"

These are the questions that made up Evie's Awesomeness form:

Can your child play sleeping tiger and other great games?

YES! Evie loves games and interacts by laughing, kicking, flapping, and moving close to us.

Does your child laugh when objects fall near her face?

YES! Evie loves when we drop cushions or soft toys beside her. She laughs when we move or tip the couch and enjoys loud noises.

Can your child play for over thirty minutes in an Excer-saucer?

YES! Evie loves being in her saucer and plays with the objects well.

Can your child play with your hair, face, and earrings?

YES! Evie will reach out to touch our face, pull my hair or earrings. She pulls very gently.

Can your child hold her legs and nearly her toes?

YES! Evie plays with her knees when she is contented and can almost reach her toes.

Can your child hold a spoon and feed herself yogurt?

YES! Evie can feed herself approx. ½ teaspoon at a time when she is in the right mood, and she can feed herself from her bottle.

Can your child roll competently?

YES! Evie is a pro roller baby! She even commando rolls in stealth mode for extra sneakiness. She will roll to get places quickly.

Can your child do sit-ups, holding her head up?

EVIE'S AWESOMENESS

YES! Evie does this exceptionally well using Dad to help her. Her record is thirteen in a row

As I answered all my questions about Evie, I noticed an easing of the helplessness and sadness weighing so heavily on me. It was replaced by excitement and joy – because, in my answers, I could see that Evie *was* growing and developing. Although her development couldn't be measured on an official chart, this *Awesomeness* form proved that she was developing in her own way and in her own time.

Instead of measuring Evie against 'normal', I measured her only against herself, and she was doing brilliantly.

Before Evie was born, I had spent four years studying at Art School in Dunedin, New Zealand, and I graduated with a Bachelor of Fine Arts, majoring in photography. During the degree, I was exposed to all kinds of art practices and had the opportunity to make art out of many different mediums. However, I discovered that no matter what medium I was working with, the theme of my work was always the same: finding beauty in brokenness and holding joy and suffering together. I would read Kahlil Gibran, Viktor Frankl and Carl Jung between classes.

I photographed usually overlooked things and created treasures out of these parts of the world. I found rich landscapes and textures hidden in dying flowers. Little feathers on muddy puddles were elevated as significant parts of the landscape that makes up the whole. I love how Marcel Proust puts it.... *"The real voyage of discovery consists, not in seeking new landscapes, but in having new eyes."* Beauty can be found everywhere if we have the eyes to seek it.

After graduation, I got married and started my own photography business. My husband and I   decided that we didn't want to have children. I wasn't the kind of person who loved being around babies or kids, and I believed there were many other ways of having meaningful connections with people and children than having kids of our own. In addition, we both valued freedom more than parenthood. And freedom for me was to avoid as many societal stereotypes and boxes as possible- to essentially live life unbound.

So, you can appreciate how shocking and difficult it was to find out I was pregnant. This wasn't the plan at all! My photography business was starting to build momentum, and the thought of having kids and living within the systems and structures of the world was terrifying to me. I was so afraid of being locked into a life of *normal*.

But then Evie was born, and all those fears disappeared. Even after we were given her dire prognosis and diagnosis, I remember thinking that she was the perfect child for us. She allowed us to live freely each day because we didn't have to follow any rules or structures. Her condition was so rare, that there was no rulebook at all. So, we could just live in the moment with her, and we appreciated every new day.

Of course, having a child with a super rare condition is not easy. It's a life full of late-night ambulance trips, a constant stream of medical appointments and the ever-present feelings of grief, fear and uncertainty.

But through all this, Evie was drawing out of me a mother I never knew existed. I was strong, resilient, gracious and joyful. She helped me to become a person I would never have imagined myself capable of becoming.

Sadly, Evie's life was not destined to be a long one. We had an incredible two and a half years with our daughter; for every one of those days, she was completely compatible with life. But, in her remarkable short life, Evie inspired a dream, which has since become part of her legacy: Super Power Baby Project.

A few years after Evie died, when I felt a bit braver and stronger, I began working on an idea that had sparked in me when Evie was still alive. I had wanted to make a book that celebrated the lives and abilities of children with chromosomal and genetic conditions. I wanted this book to be big, colourful, and beautiful. I'd never made a book before and didn't know anything about publishing, but one step at a time, one interview at a time, Super Power Baby Project was brought to life.

I found myself in homes across New Zealand, speaking with parents of children similar to Evie. They shared their stories, I photographed their children, and we laughed and cried together. I could feel the impact of Evie's life beginning to flourish.

The parents loved having a space to gush about their children. They told me that being encouraged to talk positively about their child was powerful and incredibly healing. Some parents admitted that our conversation was the first time they'd ever spoken positively about their child out loud. They'd felt trapped in the world of their child's diagnosis, of the medical words and deficits. They had felt that same hopelessness and exhaustion I had felt. The constant questions of strangers that saw difference as wrong, the comparison to normal, and the tick-box measuring scales. We all realised we weren't alone.

As I was interviewing the families, I noticed consistent themes in how the parents described their child's impact on their family and the characteristics the child possessed. For example, the parents used words like *unconditional love, perseverance, empathy, compassion, and incredible joy*. These words are some of humanity's highest ideals and the things the world needs most, and these children are the teachers of these values.

In our culture's relentless obsession with perfection and our desire to follow society's pre-prescribed measures of success, we are reducing our capacity to cultivate and embrace these ideals.

My hope in creating Super Power Baby Project was to reframe difference, celebrate humanity,   share stories and uniqueness and capture the beauty that each child possessed.

"All infants carry with them into this life, individualities and uniqueness. Amongst the uncertainties about health, development and longevity, the special strengths of such children can be discounted and ignored. No genetic test can predict anyone's personality, talents, and temperament. The discovery of those dimensions to each human life remains the special joy that each parent looks to with anticipation and wonder." – Prof Stephen Robertson

This statement, written by our own clinical geneticist in the foreword of Super Power Baby Project, encourages us to live in the realms of extraordinary and elegantly proclaims what I deeply believe about life:

None of us can be diagnosed with our identity.

RACHEL CALLANDER

The power in Rachel's story is not in how close to death she's come, but how close to life. She's been described as a great leveller of people.

Rachel is an author of two books, an award-winning artist, speaker and advocate. She is deeply passionate about the dynamics of interpersonal relationships and teaches about effective communication as the necessary skill in understanding others, drawing out their strengths and embodying connection in high context cultures.

She brings art, science and lived experience to help people collaborate effectively, achieve positive outcomes, feel seen, heard and understood and communicate clearly.

Rachel shares the legacy of her daughter Evie in many aspects of her work and life.

Find and connect with Rachel here:
www.rachelcallander.com
www.superpowerbabyproject.org

ABOUT THE PUBLISHER

As an international best-selling author, and a two-decade career in the communications, PR and media industries, Georgia Hansen founded GM House of Publishing in 2022 after realising it is part of her purpose to illuminate other's stories.

She is trained as an intuitive guide and uses this alongside her deep understanding of human communication, connection and collaboration to extract and amplify the voices of change-agents and impact makers who are ready to be seen and heard.

Her professional experience is vast, however it is her life's experiences that have catalysed her to be the voice and changemaker for other women. After losing her daughter in 2017 in a full-term stillbirth, she has been sharing and advocating for angel mamas, and recently launched Angel Mama House to support women in ways that haven't existed before, and to shift the paradigm around loss and grief.

Find out more about Georgie and her work in the world here

www.gm-house.com

www.angelmamahouse.com

"Heroes are ordinary people who make themselves extraordinary" –
Gerard Way

www.ingramcontent.com/pod-product-compliance
Lightning Source LLC
Chambersburg PA
CBHW072148090426
42741CB00025B/2974